MINOR AND SHORT FORMS OF PUBLIC WORKS CONTRACTS DESIGNED BY THE EMPLOYER

EXPLAINED

MINOR AND SHORT FORMS OF PUBLIC WORKS CONTRACTS DESIGNED BY THE EMPLOYER

EXPLAINED

By
James Howley
&
Martin Lang

CLARUS
PRESS

Published by
Clarus Press Ltd,
Griffith Campus,
South Circular Road,
Dublin 8.

Typeset by
Compuscript Ltd,
Shannon Industrial Estate,
Shannon,
Co. Clare.

Printed by
Eprint Ltd, Dublin 15

Front Cover Photography
Gerry O'Leary © www.gerryoleary.com

ISBN
978-1-905536-28-3

A CIP catalogue record for this book is available from the British Library.

All materials reproduced with the kind permission of the Oireachtas and Department of Finance
who hold copyright in the rules and forms ©

Disclaimer
Whilst every effort has been made to ensure that the contents of this book are
accurate, neither the publisher, editor or contributors can accept responsibility for
any errors or omissions or loss occasioned to any person acting or refraining from
acting as result of any material in this publication.

ABOUT THE AUTHORS

James Howley MSc, Dip Arb, Dip Proj Mgmt, MRICS, ASCS, FCIOB, FCIArb., Chartered Arbitrator, Chartered Surveyor, Accredited Adjudicator, CIArb Accredited Mediator has over 30 years experience in the construction industry. In addition to building and civil engineering contractors, he has worked with professional consultancy practices. His experience includes large-scale building and civil engineering projects, including utilities, rail, roads, oil and power generating projects in Ireland, the UK, mainland Europe and the Middle East.

He holds an MSc in Construction Law and Arbitration from Kings College, London and has completed formal training in arbitration, adjudication and mediation. He is currently working in private practice as a Construction Contracts Consultant, Arbitrator, Conciliator and Adjudicator.

Martin Lang MCIArb, CIArb Accredited Mediator has been involved in the construction industry at senior management level for the last 35 years. He began his career as an estimator and trained as a Quantity Surveyor in Dublin. He went on to be a Contracts Manager and Contracts Director with some of Ireland's leading Civil Engineering and Construction Companies. He has had an extensive career in Project Management in the United Kingdom, Spain, Portugal, the Middle East and West Africa. He joined the Construction Industry Federation in 1995 as an Executive Officer where he is now Head of Contracts. Martin has dealt with over 200 construction mediations and conciliations. Martin is also a Member of the Chartered Institute of Arbitrators, Chartered Institute of Arbitrators Accredited Mediator, Chartered Institute of Arbitrators and Engineers Ireland Assessed Conciliator, Trained Quantity Surveyor, Contract Claims Advisor, Conflict and Dispute Management Accredited Trainer, National Registered Trainer, Practicing Mediator and Conciliator. Construction Industry Management and Contracting Background, Lecturer in Construction Management and Contract Administration and an Author and Columnist.

PREFACE

It is envisaged that the Public Procurement will be the major activity sector of the construction for the foreseeable future. A large proportion of Public Sector Construction Projects will be procured under the Public Works Contract for Minor Civil Engineering and Building Works designed by the Employer for contracts less than €5 million and the Short Form of Public Works Contract for Building and Civil Engineering Works for contracts less than €500,000.00.

Construction projects, as a result of their inherent nature, can be subject to cost and time overruns. With a large financial outlay and exposure to cost and time overruns, the government require more price and time certainties on public construction projects.

The new Public Works Contracts set out strict criteria for the award of extensions of time to the project and increases to the contract sum. The contracts introduce "condition precedent" and time bar clauses whereby a contractor's claims has to be notified and submitted within a specified time period if the claims are to succeed. This new criteria introduces a new environment under which contractors must carry out business. It is important that contractors operating under these forms of construction contracts are aware of the contractual stipulations that must be completed so that contractual entitlements are not compromised.

This book has four parts: Part 1 —Public Works Contract for Minor Building and Civil Engineering Works Designed by The Employer; Part 2—Public Works Contracts Model Forms; Part 3—Letters and Notices for Contractors Using Public Works Contracts for Building and Civil Engineering Works Designed by the Employer and; Part 4—Short Public Works Contract for Civil Engineering and Building Works Designed by the Employer.

This book is set out in a clause by clause format, followed by PV1, and the Schedule where applicable.

CONTENTS

Contents for Part I

AGREEMENT 7

CONDITIONS 15

1. THE CONTRACT...15
   1.1 Definitions 15
   1.2 Interpretation 18
   1.3 Inconsistencies 19
   1.4 Pricing Document and Works Proposals 19
   1.5 Performance Bond 19
   1.6 (Sub-clause not used)...20
   1.7 Joint Ventures..20
   1.8 Assignment 20
   1.9 Miscellaneous 20

2. THE LAW 21
   2.1 Law Governing the Contract 21
   2.2 Compliance with Legal Requirements..21
   2.3 Consents 21
   2.4 Project Supervisor..21
   2.5 Safety, Health and Welfare at Work Act 2005 and Safety, Health and Welfare
       at Work (Construction) Regulations 2006 22
   2.6 Ethics in Public Office 22

3. LOSS, DAMAGE AND INJURY 24
   3.1 Employer's Risks of Loss and Damage to the Works 24
   3.2 Care of the Works 24
   3.3 Insurance of the Works and Other Risk Items 25
   3.4 Contractor's Indemnity..25
   3.5 Employer's Indemnity 25
   3.6 Public Liability and Employer's Liability Insurances 26
   3.7 Professional Indemnity Insurance 26
   3.8 Existing Facilities and Use or Occupation by Employer 26
   3.9 General Requirements Concerning Insurance 26

4. MANAGEMENT...28
   4.1 Co-operation 28
   4.2 Contractor's Representative and Supervisor...28
   4.3 Employer's Representative 29
   4.4 Employer's Representative's Communications 29
   4.5 Instructions 30
   4.6 Works Proposals..31
   4.7 Required Contractor Submissions 31
   4.8 (Sub-clause not used) 32
   4.9 Programme 32
   4.10 Progress Reports..33
   4.11 Notice and Time for Employer's Obligations 33
   4.12 Documents 34
   4.13 Contractor's Management 34
   4.14 Communications 35

    4.15   Meetings 35
    4.16   Confidentiality and Secrecy 36
    4.17   Contractor's Things Not to Be Removed 36
    4.18   Contractor's Documents 37

5.   CONTRACTOR'S PERSONNEL 38
    5.1   Contractor's Personnel to Carry Out Contractor's Obligations 38
    5.2   Qualifications and Competence 38
    5.3   Pay and Conditions of Employment 38
    5.4   Subcontractors and Specialists 39
    5.5   Collateral Warranties 41
    5.6   Removal of Work Persons 41

6.   PROPERTY 42
    6.1   Ownership of Works Items 42
    6.2   Infringement of Property Rights 42
    6.3   Works Requirements 42
    6.4   Rights in Contractor's Documents 43

7.   THE SITE 44
    7.1   Lands Made Available for the Works 44
    7.2   Trespassers 45
    7.3   Contractor Responsible for All Site Operations 45
    7.4   Services for Employer's Facilities 45
    7.5   Security and Safety of the Site and Nuisance 45
    7.6   Other Contractors 46
    7.7   Setting Out the Works 46
    7.8   Archaeological Objects and Human Remains 46
    7.9   Access and Facilities 47
    7.10   (Sub-clause not used) 47
    7.11   (Sub-clause not used) 47
    7.12   Charges 47

8.   QUALITY, TESTING AND DEFECTS 48
    8.1   Standards of Workmanship and Works Items 48
    8.2   Quality Assurance 48
    8.3   Inspection 48
    8.4   Tests 49
    8.5   Defects 49
    8.6   Defects Period 50
    8.7   Defects Certificate 51

9.   TIME AND COMPLETION 52
    9.1   Starting Date 52
    9.2   Suspension 53
    9.3   Delay and Extension of Time 53
    9.4   Programme Contingency 55
    9.5   Omissions and Reduction of Time 55
    9.6   Substantial Completion 56
    9.7   (Sub-clause not used) 56
    9.8   Liquidated Damages 56

10. CLAIMS AND ADJUSTMENTS 58
    10.1   Compensation Event 58
    10.2   Contractor to Pay Employer's Cost of Checking Quantities 58
    10.3   Contractor Claims 58
    10.4   Proposed Instructions 60
    10.5   Employer's Representative's Determination 61

	10.6	Adjustments to the Contract Sum	61
	10.7	Delay Cost	62
	10.8	Price Variation	63
	10.9	Employer's Claims	63

11. PAYMENT **65**

	11.1	Interim Payment	65
	11.2	Unfixed Works Items	66
	11.3	Retention	67
	11.4	Full Payment	67
	11.5	Final Statement	68
	11.6	Time for Payment and Interest	70
	11.7	Value Added Tax	70
	11.8	Withholding Tax	70

12. TERMINATION **71**

	12.1	Termination on Contractor Default	71
	12.2	Consequences of Default Termination	72
	12.3	Suspension by the Contractor	74
	12.4	Termination by the Contractor	74
	12.5	Termination at Employer's Election	75
	12.6	Consequences of Termination by Contractor or at Employer's Election	75
	12.7	Survival	76
	12.8	Payment	76
	12.9	Reference to Conciliation	76

13. DISPUTES **78**

	13.1	Conciliation	78
	13.2	Arbitration	79
	13.3	Jurisdiction	79
	13.4	Agent for Service	79
	13.5	Continuing Obligations	80

PV1. PRICE VARIATION **81**

	PV1.1	Contract Sum Adjustment	81
	PV1.2	Communications	82
	PV1.3	Compensation Events	82
	PV1.4	Efficiency	83
	PV1.5	Certificates & Payment	83

SCHEDULE **85**

Contents for Part II

1.	Form of tender	104
2.	Form of bid bond	107
3.	Form of letter to apparently unsuccessful tender	108
4.	Form of letter of intent	109
5.	Form of letter of acceptance	110
6.	Form of performance bond	111
7.	Form of parent company guarantee	113
8.	Form of novation and guarantee deed	116

9.   Form of appointment of project supervisor for construction stage only 120

10. Form of appointment of project supervisor for construction stage and design process 122

11. Form of appointment of project supervisor for design process only 124

12. Form of professional indemnity insurance certificate 126

13. Form of collateral warranty 128

14. Form of novation agreement 131

15. Form of rates of pay and conditions of employment certificate 133

16. Form of bond – unfixed works items 134

17. Form of retention bond 136

18. Form of conciliator's agreement 137

19. Form of bond – conciliator's recommendation 139

Contents for Part III

Letters and Notices for Contractors Using Public Works Contracts for Building
and Civil Engineering Works Designed by the Employer 141

Contents for Part IV

Short Public Works Contract for Civil Engineering and Building Works
Designed by the Employer 153

INDEX 181

PART I: PUBLIC WORKS CONTRACT FOR MINOR BUILDING AND CIVIL ENGINEERING WORKS DESIGNED BY THE EMPLOYER

CONTENTS FOR PART I

AGREEMENT 7

CONDITIONS 15

1. THE CONTRACT...15
   1.1 Definitions..15
   1.2 Interpretation 18
   1.3 Inconsistencies 19
   1.4 Pricing Document and Works Proposals 19
   1.5 Performance Bond...19
   1.6 (Sub-clause not used) 20
   1.7 Joint Ventures..20
   1.8 Assignment 20
   1.9 Miscellaneous..20

2. THE LAW 21
   2.1 Law Governing the Contract 21
   2.2 Compliance with Legal Requirements..21
   2.3 Consents..21
   2.4 Project Supervisor..21
   2.5 Safety, Health and Welfare at Work Act 2005 and Safety, Health and Welfare
       at Work (Construction) Regulations 2006 22
   2.6 Ethics in Public Office 22

3. LOSS, DAMAGE AND INJURY 24
   3.1 Employer's Risks of Loss and Damage to the Works 24
   3.2 Care of the Works 24
   3.3 Insurance of the Works and Other Risk Items 25
   3.4 Contractor's Indemnity...25
   3.5 Employer's Indemnity...25
   3.6 Public Liability and Employer's Liability Insurances 26
   3.7 Professional Indemnity Insurance 26
   3.8 Existing Facilities and Use or Occupation by Employer 26
   3.9 General Requirements Concerning Insurance 26

4. MANAGEMENT 28
   4.1 Co-operation 28
   4.2 Contractor's Representative and Supervisor..28
   4.3 Employer's Representative 29
   4.4 Employer's Representative's Communications 29
   4.5 Instructions 30
   4.6 Works Proposals...31
   4.7 Required Contractor Submissions 31
   4.8 (Sub-clause not used) 32
   4.9 Programme 32
   4.10 Progress Reports...33
   4.11 Notice and Time for Employer's Obligations 33
   4.12 Documents 34
   4.13 Contractor's Management 34
   4.14 Communications 35
   4.15 Meetings..35
   4.16 Confidentiality and Secrecy 36
   4.17 Contractor's Things Not to Be Removed 36
   4.18 Contractor's Documents..37

5.   CONTRACTOR'S PERSONNEL 38
     5.1   Contractor's Personnel to Carry Out Contractor's Obligations 38
     5.2   Qualifications and Competence 38
     5.3   Pay and Conditions of Employment..38
     5.4   Subcontractors and Specialists 39
     5.5   Collateral Warranties 41
     5.6   Removal of Work Persons..41

6.   PROPERTY 42
     6.1   Ownership of Works Items 42
     6.2   Infringement of Property Rights...42
     6.3   Works Requirements...42
     6.4   Rights in Contractor's Documents 43

7.   THE SITE..44
     7.1   Lands Made Available for the Works..44
     7.2   Trespassers...45
     7.3   Contractor Responsible for All Site Operations 45
     7.4   Services for Employer's Facilities...45
     7.5   Security and Safety of the Site and Nuisance...45
     7.6   Other Contractors 46
     7.7   Setting Out the Works..46
     7.8   Archaeological Objects and Human Remains 46
     7.9   Access and Facilities...47
     7.10 (Sub-clause not used) 47
     7.11 (Sub-clause not used) 47
     7.12 Charges...47

8.   QUALITY, TESTING AND DEFECTS..48
     8.1   Standards of Workmanship and Works Items 48
     8.2   Quality Assurance..48
     8.3   Inspection 48
     8.4   Tests..49
     8.5   Defects...49
     8.6   Defects Period..50
     8.7   Defects Certificate 51

9.   TIME AND COMPLETION...52
     9.1   Starting Date..52
     9.2   Suspension...53
     9.3   Delay and Extension of Time 53
     9.4   Programme Contingency..55
     9.5   Omissions and Reduction of Time 55
     9.6   Substantial Completion..56
     9.7   (Sub-clause not used) 56
     9.8   Liquidated Damages 56

10. CLAIMS AND ADJUSTMENTS..58
     10.1 Compensation Event..58
     10.2 Contractor to Pay Employer's Cost of Checking Quantities.........................58
     10.3 Contractor Claims 58
     10.4 Proposed Instructions 60
     10.5 Employer's Representative's Determination..61
     10.6 Adjustments to the Contract Sum 61
     10.7 Delay Cost...62
     10.8 Price Variation 63
     10.9 Employer's Claims 63

11. PAYMENT 65
    11.1 Interim Payment 65
    11.2 Unfixed Works Items 66
    11.3 Retention 67
    11.4 Full Payment 67
    11.5 Final Statement 68
    11.6 Time for Payment and Interest 70
    11.7 Value Added Tax 70
    11.8 Withholding Tax 70

12. TERMINATION 71
    12.1 Termination on Contractor Default 71
    12.2 Consequences of Default Termination 72
    12.3 Suspension by the Contractor 74
    12.4 Termination by the Contractor 74
    12.5 Termination at Employer's Election 75
    12.6 Consequences of Termination by Contractor or at Employer's Election............75
    12.7 Survival 76
    12.8 Payment 76
    12.9 Reference to Conciliation 76

13. DISPUTES 78
    13.1 Conciliation..78
    13.2 Arbitration 79
    13.3 Jurisdiction...79
    13.4 Agent for Service 79
    13.5 Continuing Obligations 80

PV1. PRICE VARIATION 81
    PV1.1 Contract Sum Adjustment 81
    PV1.2 Communications 82
    PV1.3 Compensation Events 82
    PV1.4 Efficiency..83
    PV1.5 Certificates & Payment..83

SCHEDULE 85

AGREEMENT

THIS AGREEMENT is made on [date] .... BETWEEN

The Employer: ....

Principal office of Employer: ....

AND

The Contractor: ....

Registered office / principal place
of business of Contractor: ....

BACKGROUND
The Employer has accepted the Contractor's tender to complete the Works, which consist, in general, of:

....

THE EMPLOYER AND THE CONTRACTOR AGREE as follows:

Article 1   The Contractor shall execute and complete the Works subject to and in accordance with the Contract and shall comply with its other obligations in the Contract.

Article 2   The Employer shall pay the Contractor the Contract Sum subject to and in accordance with the Contract and shall comply with its other obligations in the Contract.

Article 3   The initial Contract Sum excluding VAT is

(insert in words) ....

(insert in figures) € ....
The initial Contract Sum is a lump sum and shall only be adjusted when the Contract says so.

Article 4   The Contractor has satisfied itself before entering into the Contract of all the circumstances that may affect the cost of executing and completing the Works and of the correctness and sufficiency of the Contract Sum to cover the cost of performing the Contract. The Contractor has included in the initial Contract Sum allowances for all risks, customs, policies, practices, and other circumstances that may affect its performance of the Contract, whether they could or could not have been foreseen, except for events for which the Contract provides for adjustment of the initial Contract Sum.

Article 5   The Contract consists of the following documents:
  • this Agreement
  • the Contractor's tender and the Letter of Acceptance and any post-tender clarifications listed in it
  • the attached Conditions and completed Schedule
  • the Works Requirements, completed Pricing Document, and Works Proposals identified in the attached Schedule

Article 6   The Contract takes effect from the Contract Date.

The Employer

Given under the Employer's seal:

Affix Employer's seal: ....

....
signatures of persons authorised to authenticate the seal

OR[1]

Signed on behalf of the Employer: ....
Signature of person authorised to sign contracts on behalf of the Employer

In the presence of:
Name of witness: ....
Signature of witness: ....
Witness's occupation: ....
Witness's address: ....

The Contractor

Given under the Contractor's common seal:[2]

Affix Contractor's common seal: ....

Signatures of persons authorised
to authenticate the seal: ....

OR

Signed, sealed and delivered by:

Name of attorney: ....

Signature of attorney: ....

As lawful attorney of the Contractor under a power of attorney dated: ....

Affix attorney's personal seal: ....

In the presence of:
Name of witness: ....
Signature of witness: ....
Witness's occupation: ....
Witness's address: ....

OR

---

[1] Execution in accordance with the legislation governing the authority, or articles of association if a company.
[2] If the Contractor is a company that is not incorporated in Ireland, execution will be in accordance with the law of its jurisdiction of incoporation for execution of a deed.

Signed on behalf of the Contractor: ....

Signature of person authorised to sign contracts on behalf of the Contractor

In the presence of

Name of witness: ....

Signature of witness: ....

Witness's occupation: ....

Witness's address: ....

OR[3]

Signed, sealed and delivered by:

Name of Contractor: ....

Signature of Contractor: ....

Affix Contractor's personal seal: ....

In the presence of:

Name of witness: ....

Signature of witness: ....

Witness's occupation: ....

Witness's address: ....

OR

Signed by:

Name of Contractor: ....

Signature of Contractor: ....

In the presence of

Name of witness: ....

Signature of witness: ....

Witness's occupation: ....

Witness's address: ....

---

[3] If the Contractor is an individual.

If the Contractor is a partnership or joint venture, execution must be by each member, using the blocks below.

Partner / Joint Venture Member 1

Given under the common seal[4] of:

Name of joint venture member: ....

Affix Contractor's common seal: ....

*Signatures of persons authorised
to authenticate the seal:* ....

OR

Signed, sealed and delivered by:
Name of attorney: ....
Signature of attorney: ....

As lawful attorney of:
Name of joint venture member: ....

under a power of attorney dated: ....
Affix attorney's personal seal: ....

In the presence of:
Name of witness: ....
Signature of witness: ....
Witness's occupation: ....
Witness's address: ....

OR

Signed on behalf of joint venture member: ....
Signature of person authorised to sign contracts on behalf of joint venture member

Name of joint venture member: ....

In the presence of
Name of witness: ....
Signature of witness: ....
Witness's occupation: ....
Witness's address: ....

---

[4] If a member of the joint venture is a company that is not incorporated in Ireland, execution will be in accordance with the law of its jurisdiction of incorporation for execution of a deed.

Partner / Joint Venture Member 2

Given under the common seal[5] of:

Name of joint venture member: ....

Affix Contractor's common seal: ....

Signatures of persons authorised
to authenticate the seal: ....

OR

Signed, sealed and delivered by:
Name of attorney: ....
Signature of attorney: ....

As lawful attorney of:
Name of joint venture member: ....

under a power of attorney dated: ....
Affix attorney's personal seal: ....

In the presence of:
Name of witness: ....
Signature of witness: ....
Witness's occupation: ....
Witness's address: ....

OR

Signed on behalf of joint venture member: ....
Signature of person authorised to sign contracts on behalf of joint venture member

Name of joint venture member: ....

In the presence of
Name of witness: ....
Signature of witness: ....
Witness's occupation: ....
Witness's address: ....

---

[5] If a member of the joint venture is a company that is not incorporated in Ireland, execution will be in accordance with the law of its jurisdiction of incorporation for execution of a deed.

Partner / Joint Venture Member 3

Given under the common seal[6] of:

Name of joint venture member: ....

Affix Contractor's common seal: ....

Signatures of persons authorised
to authenticate the seal: ....

OR

Signed, sealed and delivered by:
Name of attorney: ....
Signature of attorney: ....

As lawful attorney of:
Name of joint venture member: ....

under a power of attorney dated: ....
Affix attorney's personal seal: ....

In the presence of:
Name of witness: ....
Signature of witness: ....
Witness's occupation: ....
Witness's address: ....

OR

Signed on behalf of joint venture member: ....
Signature of person authorised to sign contracts on behalf of joint venture member

Name of joint venture member: ....

In the presence of
Name of witness: ....
Signature of witness: ....
Witness's occupation: ....
Witness's address: ....

---

[6] If a member of the joint venture is a company that is not incorporated in Ireland, execution will be in accordance with the law of its jurisdiction of incorporation for execution of a deed.

Any additional required execution blocks should be inserted below.

GENERAL NOTE

The first part of the contract sets out the Articles of Agreement. This is the basic contract and describes what the Contractor agrees to do and the price the Employer agrees to pay to the Contractor. The Articles of Agreement set out the fundamental relationship between the Contractor and the Employer.

There are six articles expressing the contract. They establish that this is a Fixed Price Lump Sum Contract and, in exchange for the contract sum, the Contractor will carry out the works in accordance with the contract documents.

Article 4 sets out that, in calculating the tender price, the Contractor has taken into account that he has included in the initial contract sum allowances for all risks, customs, policies, practices, and other circumstances that may affect its performance of the contract, whether they could or could not have been foreseen, except for events for which the contract provides for adjustment of the initial contract sum.

The contract allows the Employer to transfer certain risks to the Contractor. These risks, 1 to 21, are detailed in Section K of the Schedule, Part 1. Item 17 should normally, but not necessarily be a compensation event. Items 18–21 should be compensation events. Therefore, risks to be assumed by the Employer are specified in the contract — the Contractor deals with everything else.

The initial contract sum is inserted as VAT exclusive and is referred to as a lump sum to be adjusted only when the contract says so.

Article 6 states that the contract takes effect from the contract date. The contract date is the date the Employer issues the "letter of acceptance".

CONDITIONS

1 THE CONTRACT

1.1 Definitions

The following terms have the following meanings in the Contract:

Term	Meaning
Change Order	an instruction of the Employer's Representative to change [including add to or omit from] the Works or to change [including impose or remove] constraints in the Contract on how the Works are to be executed.
Consent	planning permission, order, approval, certificate, fire certificate, licence, permit, environmental impact statement, or other consent required by Law for the execution or completion of the Works, or identified as a Consent in the Works Requirements.
Contract Date	the date the Employer issued the Letter of Acceptance.
Contract Sum	the amount identified in the Agreement as the initial Contract Sum, as adjusted in accordance with the Contract.
Contractor's Documents	drawings, specifications, manuals, reports and other [eye readables and machine readable] written material relating to the Works that the Contractor uses, prepares or gives to the Employer or any other person, or is to use, prepare or give to the Employer or any other person • under the Works Requirements or • under any Legal Requirement or • to obtain any Consent.

NOTE

"Contractor's Documents" mean drawings, specifications, manuals, reports and other written material relating to the works. This could be the Contractor's applications for consents under the contract for which he may be responsible. Such responsibilities will be contained within the contract documents.

Contractor's Things	equipment, facilities and other things the Contractor [or Contractor's Personnel] uses on or adjacent to the Site to execute the Works, except Works Items.
Contractor's Personnel	the Contractor's representative, supervisor and Subcontractors, employees and other persons working on or adjacent to the Site for the Contractor or Subcontractors, and other persons assisting the Contractor to perform the Contract.
Date for Substantial Completion of the Works or a Section	the date identified as the Date for Substantial Completion of the Works or Section in the Schedule, part 1G or 2C, and, if the Schedule states a period, the last day of that period, starting on the Contract Date, in either case as adjusted in accordance with the Contract.
Defect	non-compliance of the Works or a Works Item with the Contract [including a failed test and, after Substantial Completion, work that has not been completed].
Defects Certificate	a certificate of the Employer's Representative that the Defects Period has ended.

Defects Period	the period starting on Substantial Completion of the Works and continuing for the period stated in the Schedule, as may be extended under sub-clause 8.6.2.
Designated Date	the date 10 days before the last day for receipt of the Contractor's tender for the Works, or, if there was none, 10 days before the Employer received the Contractor's tender for the Works.
Employer's Personnel	any of the following:

- the Employer's Representative

- the Employer's employees, agents and consultants in connection with the Contract when acting on behalf of the Employer but not when exercising authority under Law

- other contractors of the Employer working on the Site when acting within the scope of their contracts with the Employer

- anyone else the Employer's Representative notifies the Contractor is Employer's Personnel.

NOTE

"Employer's Personnel" can also include other Contractors engaged by the Employer on the site.

Employer's Representative	the engineer, architect, quantity surveyor or other person appointed by the Employer as its representative in accordance with the Contract.
Law	enactments and statutory instruments, each as defined by the Interpretation Act 2005, and regulations, directives and decisions of the European Union having direct effect in Ireland.
Legal Requirement	a requirement that applies to the Works as a result of any of the following:

- Law

- a Consent

- a decision of an Irish court, the European Court of Justice or the European Court of First Instance

- the requirements of any person having authority in connection with the Works under any Law

- the requirements of any person with whose systems the Works will connect

- the legal rights of any person.

Letter of Acceptance	the Employer's letter to the Contractor accepting the Contractor's tender.
Section	a part of the Works identified as a Section in the Schedule, part 1G.
Site	any place

- where the Works are to be executed according to the Contract or

- provided by the Employer for the Works or

- where the Contractor is to operate or maintain Employer's facilities or

- that the Works Requirements identify as part of the Site.

Site Working Day	a day on which, according to the Contract and the Contractor's programme most recently submitted to the Employer's Representative, the Contractor is to execute the Works on the Site.

NOTE

"Site Working Day", as opposed to "working day", is a day indicted to be a working day by the last accepted programme. It is an important definition as it is only site working days for which an extension of time can be allowed. It has a particular effect on claims occurring during a holiday period: if they are not taken for in the programme they may be ignored in the calculation of the extension of time.

Specialist	any of the following:

- a Subcontractor or supplier of a Works Item named in the Contract

- Contractor's Personnel who do or are to do design

- Contractor's Personnel stated in the Works Requirements to be Specialists.

Starting Date	the day the Contractor proposes to start executing the Works, as notified by the Contractor to the Employer's Representative under sub-clause 9.1.
Subcontractor	a person to whom the execution of part of the Works is subcontracted [by the Contractor or another Subcontractor].
Substantial Completion of the Works or a Section	all of the following have happened:

(1)   the Works or Section are complete so that they can be taken over and used by the Employer for their intended purpose and there are no Defects other than

    (a)   Defects accepted by the Employer under sub-clause 8.5.4 or

    (b)   minor Defects to which all of the following apply:

        (i)   they do not prevent the Works or the part from being used for their intended purpose

        (ii)   the Employer's Representative considers the Contractor has reasonable grounds for not promptly rectifying them

        (iii)   rectification will not prejudice the safe and convenient use of the Works or the part

(2)   all tests that are required by the Contract to be passed before Substantial Completion have been passed

(3)   the Contractor has given the Employer's Representative the Contractor's Documents that the Contract requires be provided before Substantial Completion

(4)   the Contractor has given the Employer's Representative the collateral warranties that the Contract requires for the Works or part.

NOTE

"Substantial Completion" includes conditions that all tests required have been completed and passed before substantial completion can occur. The Contractor must provide the documents as required by the contract to the Employer or Employer's Representative including all collateral warranties before substantial completion can occur. Management and production of all such documentation is essential for the Contractor.

VAT	value-added tax payable in Ireland under Law.
Works Item	a part of the Works, anything that the Contractor intends will become part of the Works, or temporary works for the Works.

1.2   Interpretation

1.2.1   The parties intend the Contract to be given purposeful meaning for efficiency and public benefit generally and as particularly identified in the Contract.

1.2.2   Unless the context indicates otherwise, in the Contract

(1)   References to the **Works** are to the works described in the Works Requirements.

(2)   Words in the singular include the plural and vice versa.

(3)   References to an **individual** are to a human person.

(4)   References to a **person** include human persons and corporate and unincorporated bodies.

(5)   Words in any gender include all genders.

(6)   References to any **Law** include amendments and replacements.

(7)   References to the **Contract** or any other writing include amendments.

(8)   References to a **day** mean a calendar day.

(9)   References to a **week** mean a period of 7 days.

(10)   References to a **month** mean a calendar month.

(11)   References to a **working day** mean a day that is not Saturday, Sunday, a public holiday established under the Organisation of Working Time Act 1997 or Good Friday.

(12)   References to a requirement to **submit** a document or proposed course of action to Employer's Representative mean to submit it according to sub-clause 4.7, or another procedure that applies according to the Works Requirements, and sub-clause 4.7 or the Works Requirements shall apply in every such case. [Accordingly the Contractor may not implement the submission until permitted by sub-clause 4.7 or the Works Requirements.]

(13)   References to the Contractor's **current programme** are to the programme in the Works Proposals, if there is one, if not, to the programme first submitted by the Contractor under sub-clause 4.9, or, in either case, to any later programme submitted by the Contractor if the period for the Employer's Representative to review it has passed and there is no outstanding objection.

(14)   References to **liability** include claims, demands and proceedings.

(15)   Terms such as **including, in particular, such as**, and **for example**, are not to be read as exhaustive, or to limit, but may extend, the generality of the provisions to which they relate.

(16)   References to the **Agreement** and **Schedule** are to the attached agreement and completed schedule.

(17)   References to the **Works Requirements, Works Proposals** and the **Pricing Document** are to the Works Requirements, Works Proposals and Pricing Document identified in the Schedule, part 1B; in the case of Works Requirements, as changed by Change Orders; and in the case of Works Proposals, as changed under sub-clause 4.6.2.

(18)   References to **Delay Events** and **Compensation Events** are to events identified as Delay Events and Compensation Events in the Schedule, part 1K.

(19)   References to the **initial** Contract Sum are to the Contract Sum stated in the Agreement; references to an initial Date for Substantial Completion are to a Date for Substantial Completion identified in the Schedule; and references to the initial Works Requirements are to the Works Requirements identified in the Schedule.

1.2.3   Clarifications, examples and reminders are included occasionally in square brackets to show that no significance is to be given to their absence elsewhere.

1.3   Inconsistencies

1.3.1   Except when the Contract states otherwise, the documents in the Contract are to be taken as mutually explanatory of each other if possible. If there is an inconsistency between the documents, they take precedence as follows:

- ○ First, the Agreement, even if it has not been executed
- ○ Second, the attached Schedule and the Letter of Acceptance and any post-tender clarifications listed in it
- ○ Third, the Contractor's completed form of tender (excluding other documents in the tender)
- ○ Fourth, these Conditions
- ○ Fifth, the Works Requirements
- ○ Sixth, the Pricing Document
- ○ Seventh, the Works Proposals, if there are any
- ○ Eighth, any other documents in the Contract

1.3.2   If either party becomes aware of any inconsistency between terms of the Contract, it shall promptly inform the other party.

1.3.3   If there is an inconsistency between figured and scaled dimensions, the figured dimensions prevail.

1.3.4   If the Works Requirements include a Bill of Quantities, and the Bill of Quantities is inconsistent with any other Works Requirements, the other Works Requirements prevail.

NOTE

Inconsistencies should be promptly notified. No action is identified in the contract, however precedence of documents applies. The status of the Bills of Quantities will be identified within the contract documents in the Schedule Part 1K.

1.4   Pricing Document and Works Proposals

Nothing in and no omission from the Pricing Document or Works Proposals limits the scope of the Works or the Contractor's obligations. Nothing in the Pricing Document or Works Proposals imposes obligations on the Employer.

1.5   Performance Bond

Before the Starting Date, unless the Schedule, part 1E, says that no bond is required, the Contractor shall give the Employer a performance bond in the form in the Works Requirements, or, if there is none, a form approved by the Employer. The performance bond shall be in the amount stated in the Schedule, part 1E, and shall be executed by the Contractor and by a surety approved by the Employer.

NOTE

Any performance bond is to be delivered before the start date notified by the Contractor. That will normally be within four weeks of the issue of the Letter of Acceptance.

Bonds and guarantees are to comply with model forms contained within the contract documents.

1.6   (Sub-clause not used)

1.7   Joint Ventures

If the Contractor is a joint venture, consortium or other unincorporated grouping of two or more persons, those persons shall be jointly and severally liable to the Employer for the performance of the Contract.

1.8   Assignment

The Contractor may not assign the benefit of the Contract, or any part of it, without the Employer's consent.

1.9   Miscellaneous

1.9.1   The Contract and the documents referred to in it supersede all previous representations, arrangements, understandings and agreements between the parties about the subject-matter of the Contract, and set out the entire agreement between the parties about the subject-matter of the Contract. Neither party has relied on any other written or oral representation, arrangement, understanding or agreement. The Employer does not warrant the correctness, completeness or suitability of any information provided to the Contractor on, before or after the Contract Date, and shall have no liability in connection with such information, except as expressly stated in the Contract.

1.9.2   All the terms of the Contract are severable, and if any part is unenforceable, illegal or void, it is to that extent considered not to form part of the Contract, and the enforceability, legality and validity of the rest of the Contract will not be affected.

1.9.3   The Contract may only be changed by a document in writing signed by an authorised representative of each party.

NOTE

This confirms that any changes to the contract documents can only be effected when made in writing by authorised persons. It is important to note clause 1.9.1 wherein it is stated "[t]he Employer does not warrant the correctness, completeness or suitability of any information provided to the Contractor on, before or after the Contract Date, and shall have no liability in connection with such information, except as expressly stated in the Contract". This means that all information provided is without warranty. Careful note of this requirement should be made by Contractors.

1.9.4   The rights of a party will not be prejudiced or restricted by any indulgence or forbearance extended to the other party, and no waiver by a party of any breach will waive any other breach. No failure or delay by a party in exercising any right or remedy will waive the right or remedy, nor will any single or partial exercise or waiver of any right or remedy prejudice any other exercise of that or any other right or remedy.

GENERAL NOTE ON SECTION

This section of the contract deals with how the parties are to read and interpret the contract and how the contract documents will be treated.

2 THE LAW

2.1 Law Governing the Contract

Irish law governs the Contract and its interpretation.

2.2 Compliance with Legal Requirements

The Contractor shall in performing the Contract comply with all Legal Requirements and ensure that the Contractor's Personnel comply with all Legal Requirements.

2.3 Consents

2.3.1 The Employer has obtained, or shall obtain, the Consents that the Works Requirements say that the Employer is to obtain. The Contractor shall obtain all other Consents.

2.3.2 The Contractor shall give and comply with all notices and pay all taxes, fees and charges required under Legal Requirements to be paid in connection with performing the Contract, unless the Works Requirements say otherwise.

> **NOTE**
>
> Careful consideration should be given to the implications of clause 2.3.1, in particular the extremely wide interpretation contained in the last sentence where the Contractor is made liable to "obtain all other consents".

2.4 Project Supervisor

2.4.1 If the Schedule, part 1C, states that the Contractor is to be appointed project supervisor for the construction stage in accordance with the Safety, Health and Welfare at Work (Construction) Regulations 2006 (the **Construction Regulations**) for the Works, or a project including the Works, the Contractor shall accept the appointment by entering into the appointment in the form in the Works Requirements. If the Schedule, part 1C, states that an individual or body corporate named in the Works Proposals is to be appointed project supervisor for the construction stage in accordance with the Construction Regulations for the Works, or a project including the Works, the Contractor shall ensure that the individual or body corporate named in the Works Proposals accepts the appointment by entering into the appointment in the form in the Works Requirements. The Contractor shall, if appointed as project supervisor, comply with its obligations under the Construction Regulations in connection with that appointment. If the Employer terminates the appointment of the Contractor or other person named in the Works Proposals as project supervisor for the construction stage as a result of that project supervisor's failure to comply with its obligations, the Contractor shall pay to the Employer all the Employer's cost resulting from the termination [including the cost of appointing and fees and expenses paid to a replacement project supervisor, or, if the Employer acts as project supervisor itself, the Employer's cost of doing so].

> **NOTE**
>
> If a Contractor takes on this role and fails to adequately perform, resource and provide the necessary insurances, the Employer may terminate the Contractor's role and appoint another party to carry out the duties of project supervisor (construction stage). In this event the Contractor is replaced in this role and the Contractor is responsible for all the Employer's costs involved in the new appointment.

2.4.2 If the Contractor or a person named in the Works Proposals is to be appointed as project supervisor for the construction stage, the Contractor represents and warrants to the Employer that the Contractor or person named in the Works Proposals is competent and will allocate adequate resources to enable itself to perform its duties under the Construction Regulations.

2.4.3 If the Contractor or a person named in the Works Proposals is appointed as project supervisor for the construction stage the Contractor shall ensure that the project supervisor has the insurances required of the project supervisor under its appointment.

NOTE

If the Employer appoints a person other than the Contractor as Project Supervisor, the Contractor is obliged to comply with all the requirements of the Project Supervisor.

2.4.4 The Contractor shall [without adjustment to the Contract Sum or extension of time] comply with all the lawful directions of the project supervisors appointed for the construction stage and the design process in accordance with the Construction Regulations for the Works, or any project including the Works, and give them any copies of Contractor's Documents that they may request.

2.4.5 The Contractor shall, before Substantial Completion of the Works or any Section, give the Employer the documents required for the safety file (as defined in the Construction Regulations).

NOTE

Failure to produce the documents necessary to complete the safety file could adversely affect the issue of the certificate for substantial completion.

2.5   Safety, Health and Welfare at Work Act 2005 and Safety, Health and Welfare at Work (Construction) Regulations 2006

2.5.1 The Contractor shall [without limiting other obligations] ensure, so far as is reasonably practicable, that the Works are constructed to be safe and without risk to health, and that the Works comply in all respects, as appropriate, with the relevant statutory provisions.

2.5.2 The Contractor represents and warrants to the Employer that the Contractor is, and will, while performing the Contract, be a competent person for the purpose of ensuring, so far as is reasonably practicable, that the Works are constructed to be safe and without risk to health and that they comply in all respects, as appropriate, with the relevant statutory provisions.

2.5.3 The Contractor represents and warrants to the Employer that the Contractor is and will, while performing the Contract, be a competent person to carry out the Works and has allocated and will allocate sufficient resources to enable itself to comply with the requirements and prohibitions imposed on the Contractor by or under the relevant statutory provisions.

2.5.4 In this sub-clause 2.5 and sub-clause 2.4, **competent person**, **reasonably practicable** and **relevant statutory provisions** are construed according to section 2 of the Safety, Health and Welfare at Work Act 2005.

2.6   Ethics in Public Office

The Contractor warrants that

2.6.1 neither the Contractor nor any person on the Contractor's behalf has offered, given or agreed to give to the Employer or to any of the Employer's Personnel any gift or consideration of any kind in connection with the Contract, nor will they make such an offer, gift or agreement and

2.6.2 neither the Contractor nor any person on the Contractor's behalf has committed any offence under the Prevention of Corruption Acts 1889 to 2001 or the Ethics in Public Office Acts 1995 and 2001 in connection with the Contract, nor will they commit any such offence and

2.6.3 no Minister of the Government or Minister of State, or officer or employee of the Employer, will have or receive any share or part of the Contract or any benefit from the Contract and

2.6.4 unless fully disclosed to and agreed by the Employer in advance

(1) no former officer nor employee of the Employer nor of a consultant to the Employer whose duties related to the Works will, for 12 months after leaving the employment or office, be engaged as Contractor's Personnel and

(2) no consultant or former consultant to the Employer whose duties related to the Works will be engaged as Contractor's Personnel, except for a Specialist whose contract is to be novated from the Employer to the Contractor.

NOTE

This sub-clause deals with ethics in public office which contain restrictions as to the employment of personnel, including consultants, who were formerly engaged on the works by the Employer. The sub-clause contains a prohibition on their working for the Contractor.

GENERAL NOTE ON SECTION

This section sets out the Contractor's legal obligation to carry out the contract in accordance with the law, legal requirements and consents obtained and to be obtained in connection with the works requirements.

This section, for the first time in Irish standard forms of construction contracts, introduce the requirements in relation to health, safety and welfare legislation. It is under this section that the risk of changes in legislation is passed to the Contractor.

It is in this section that the risks of consents are transferred to the Contractor. The Contractor shall be informed of the consents for which the Employer will be responsible. All other consents will be the responsibility of the Contractor including costs both of obtaining the consents themselves and any delay incurred while awaiting the consents.

3 LOSS, DAMAGE AND INJURY

3.1 Employer's Risks of Loss and Damage to the Works

The Employer shall bear the risk of loss of or damage to the Works resulting from any of the following:

(1) war, invasion, act of foreign enemies, hostilities whether war is declared or not, civil war, rebellion, revolution, insurrection, military or usurped power

(2) pressure waves caused by aircraft or other airborne objects travelling at sonic or supersonic speeds

(3) contamination by radioactivity or radioactive, toxic, explosive or other hazardous properties of any explosive nuclear assembly or its components, in each case not caused by the Contractor or the Contractor's Personnel

(4) terrorism, but only if terrorism is a permitted exclusion from the Contractor's insurance of the Works

(5) use or occupation of the Works by the Employer or the Employer's Personnel, other than

   (i) as provided for in the Contract or

   (ii) to the extent that the loss or damage is caused by the negligence of the Contractor or the Contractor's Personnel, or the Contractor's breach of the Contract (subject to sub-clause 3.8 if it applies)

(6) design of the Works by the Employer or Employer's Personnel, but not if the design is covered by insurance required under the Contract.

3.2 Care of the Works

3.2.1 The Contractor shall have full responsibility for the care of, and risk of loss of and damage to, the Works, Works Items, Contractor's Things, Works Requirements, Works Proposals, Contractor's Documents, and anything the Employer gives the Contractor for the Works (together, **Risk Items**) from and including the Starting Date until and including the date the Employer's Representative issues the certificate of Substantial Completion of the Works or relevant Section. After that date, the Contractor shall be responsible for loss of and damage to Risk Items due to any of the following:

   (1) Defects

   (2) occurrences before the Employer's Representative issued the certificate of Substantial Completion

   (3) activities of the Contractor or Contractor's Personnel.

But the Contractor's responsibility under this sub-clause 3.2 excludes loss of and damage to the Works that is at the Employer's risk under sub-clause 3.1.

3.2.2 The Contractor shall promptly rectify any loss and damage to Risk Items for which it is responsible under this sub-clause 3.2 [at its own expense if there are not sufficient insurance proceeds].

3.2.3 If loss of or damage to the Works, for which the Contractor is not responsible under this sub-clause 3.2, occurs before the Defects Certificate is issued, the Contractor shall rectify it in accordance with any instruction of the Employer.

3.3 Insurance of the Works and Other Risk Items

3.3.1 From the Starting Date, the Contractor shall insure the Works and other Risk Items against loss and damage. The insurance shall name the Contractor, the Employer and any other persons the Employer requires as co-insured. The insurance shall be kept in place for each Section until the date that the certificate of Substantial Completion of the Section is issued, and for the Works, except Sections that have a certificate of Substantial Completion, until the date that the certificate of Substantial Completion of the Works is issued. If so required in the Schedule, part 1D, the insurance for any Section or part of the Works that has reached Substantial Completion shall be extended until the Employer's Representative certifies Substantial Completion of the whole of the Works. In any event, after Substantial Completion, the insurance shall be kept in place until the Defects Certificate is issued, to cover loss and damage for which the Contractor remains responsible under the Contract. The limit of the insurance shall be, except for loss of or damage to Contractor's Things, for the full reinstatement cost of the property insured, including the cost of demolition, removal of debris, delivery, professional fees, inflation occurring during the construction and reinstatement periods, and profit. The sum insured for professional fees shall include at least the percentage of the Contract Sum stated in the Schedule, part 1D.

3.3.2 The proceeds of the insurance of the Works, less the portion to cover professional fees that the Employer is to pay, shall be paid into a bank account in the joint names of the Employer and the Contractor. They shall be paid out of the account to the Contractor in instalments on the basis of interim payment certificates of the Employer's Representative of the Contract value of the work done and Works Items delivered to the Site to rectify the loss or damage, following generally sub-clause 11.1, and also paid out of the account to the Employer for its other costs. Any balance remaining in the account after the work of rectification is complete shall be paid to the Employer.

3.4 Contractor's Indemnity

3.4.1 The Contractor shall indemnify the Employer and the Employer's employees against

(1) liability and

(2) loss of and damage to the Employer's property [including the Site], unless excluded under sub-clause 3.8 arising from or in the course of the Contractor's performance or non-performance of the Contract.

3.4.2 The Contractor's indemnity in this sub-clause 3.4 does not apply to the Employer's liability under the Contract to the Contractor; nor does it apply to liability to the extent that the liability is covered by the Employer's indemnities in sub-clauses 3.5 and 6.2.

3.4.3 The Contractor's indemnity for liability for death, injury or illness of any Contractor's Personnel shall apply regardless of whether the death, illness or injury was caused wholly or in part by the negligence of the Employer or any Employer's Personnel.

3.5 Employer's Indemnity

The Employer shall indemnify the Contractor against liability the Contractor incurs in the course of performing the Contract, to the extent that the liability is

(1) caused by the negligence of the Employer or

(2) for property damage that is the unavoidable result of executing the Works in accordance with the Works Requirements.

But this indemnity does not cover liability for death, injury or illness of Contractor's Personnel.

3.6   Public Liability and Employer's Liability Insurances

3.6.1   From the Starting Date until the date the Defects Certificate is issued, the Contractor shall insure the Employer and the Contractor as co-insured against their respective liabilities for

(1)   death, injury or illness of any person and

(2)   loss of or damage to any physical property and

(3)   obstruction, loss of amenities, nuisance, trespass, stoppage of traffic and infringement of light, easement or quasi-easement resulting from an accident arising from or in the course of the performance or non-performance of the Contract.

3.6.2   From the Starting Date until the date the Defects Certificate is issued, the Contractor shall insure itself against liability for death, injury or illness of Contractor's Personnel. For employees of Subcontractors, this obligation may be satisfied by ensuring that the Subcontractor maintains the insurance. The Contractor shall ensure that this insurance includes a provision that indemnifies the Employer against any liability for which the Contractor would be entitled to an indemnity, including costs, charges and expenses.

3.6.3   The minimum indemnity limit of the Contractor's public liability and employer's liability insurances shall be as stated in the Schedule, part 1D.

3.6.4   If the Contractor or the Contractor's Personnel return to the Site in connection with the Works after the Defects Certificate is issued, the Contractor shall ensure the insurances required by this sub-clause 3.6 are in place at all times that the Contractor or Contractor's Personnel are on Site.

3.7   Professional Indemnity Insurance

If the Schedule states that professional indemnity insurance is required, from the Starting Date until the sixth anniversary of the date that the Employer's Representative certifies Substantial Completion of the Works, or any other period stated in the Schedule, part 1D, the Contractor shall maintain professional indemnity insurance for its performance of the Contract. The indemnity limit shall be at least that stated in the Schedule, part 1D. This insurance shall include retroactive cover to when the Contractor's design of the Works and Works Items started.

3.8   Existing Facilities and Use or Occupation by Employer

This sub-clause 3.8 shall apply only if so stated in the Schedule, part 1D. To the extent that the Works involve alteration or extension of existing facilities owned by the Employer, and to the extent that the Employer uses or occupies the Works, the Employer shall bear the risk of loss of or damage to those facilities and the part of the Works used or occupied by the Employer, and their contents owned by the Employer, caused by any of the following perils, as defined in the Works Requirements or, if not defined there, in standard fire and specified perils insurance policies available in Ireland:

(1)   fire, storm, tempest, flood

(2)   bursting or overflowing of water tanks, apparatus or pipes

(3)   explosion, impact, aircraft

(4)   riot, civil commotion or malicious damage.

3.9   General Requirements Concerning Insurance

3.9.1   The insurance required by the Contract (the **Insurance**) shall be placed with reputable insurers approved by the Employer.

3.9.2   The only exclusions from the Insurance shall be those listed in the Schedule, part 1D. The levels of excess shall be no higher than stated in the Schedule, part 1D.

3.9.3 Liability Insurance on which the Employer is required to be co-insured shall include a cross liability clause. All Insurance on which the Employer is required to be co-insured shall provide that

(1) the insurer accepts the term "insured" as applying to each insured person as if a separate policy of insurance had been issued to each of them, but without the overall limit of indemnity being increased as a result, and that non-compliance by the Contractor or any other co-insured will not affect the Employer's rights and

(2) the insurer agrees to waive all rights of subrogation or action against any of the persons who are insured.

3.9.4 The Contractor shall comply with the terms of the Insurance policies.

3.9.5 Within 10 working days of being requested to do so, the Contractor shall give the Employer evidence to the Employer's satisfaction that the Insurances are in effect, including copies of policies and receipts for premiums. For professional indemnity insurance, a certificate in the form included in the Works Requirements, or, if there is none, a form approved by the Employer, signed by the broker or underwriter, may be given instead of a copy of the professional indemnity policy.

3.9.6 The Contractor shall not make any material reduction to the Insurance cover unless approved in advance by the Employer. The Contractor shall promptly notify the Employer of any cancellation, renewal, non-renewal or material reduction by the insurer of any Insurance policy.

3.9.7 If the Contractor fails to maintain any of the Insurances in the terms required by the Contract, the Employer shall be entitled [without affecting its other rights] to take out the insurance and pay the premiums, and the Contractor shall pay the amount of the premiums to the Employer on demand.

GENERAL NOTE ON SECTION

This section of the Contract sets out the risks each party will bear in respect of loss or damage to the works and includes the insurance requirements and the Contractor's obligation to take care of the works, both during the life of the project and after practical completion until the Defects Certificate is issued by the Employer's Representative.

The indemnities to be provided by the Contractor and the Employer are detailed, including the fact that the Employer may require professional indemnity cover for any element of design to be carried out by the Contractor his personnel.

The definition of "liability" under this contract is broad. It is possible that the indemnity provisions may extend to a Contractor's liability to consequential and indirect losses incurred. Contractors should seek advice from their brokers or insurance agents on these provisions.

The Contractor must have the required insurances in place before the start date. Evidence of such has to be produced within 10 working days of a request from the Employer, including copies of policies and receipts for premiums paid. From a contract-administration point of view, no change in insurance levels is allowed without advance notice and approval from the Employer. The Employer, on default, can take out his own insurance and recover the cost from the Contractor. The Employer may require the Contractor to extend his "all risks" insurance to cover the Employer's own facilities and contents for standard perils. Contractors should note that terrorism and asbestos indemnities may be listed as possible exclusions.

4   MANAGEMENT

4.1   Co-operation

4.1.1   The Employer [subject to restraints as a public authority] and the Contractor shall support reciprocal co-operation for the Contract purposes, including co-operation with and between Contractor's Personnel and Employer's Personnel.

4.1.2   Such support may be relevant particularly to any of the following:

(1)   negotiation of agreements provided for in the Contract

(2)   use of most effective and compatible electronic and other methods of communicating and recording

(3)   efficient order and timing of information provided for in the Contract

(4)   minimising the effects of suspension

(5)   efforts by the Contractor to minimise delay and Compensation Events and their effects

(6)   Contractor's flexible management

4.1.3   Either party, or the Employer's Representative, may request clarifications, consultations, workshops, exchange of information and expertise, or investigations, although not provided for elsewhere in the Contract. The request shall specify purposes and, as relevant, proposed participants, arrangements, methods and any proposals for recording or agreeing results.

NOTE

This sub-clause provides a useful facility to have all matters, or any contentious matters, examined to determine the basis of any instruction or decision of the Employer's Representative and to examine whether the Contractor has any entitlements arising from the determination of the Employer's Representative.

4.1.4   The parties may agree to consult or communicate, without prejudice. In any case, offering or giving co-operation does not imply any admission of any responsibility or alter either party's rights or duties unless otherwise agreed in writing.

4.2   Contractor's Representative and Supervisor

4.2.1   The Contractor shall appoint, before the Starting Date

(1)   a representative with full authority to act on behalf of the Contractor in all matters concerning the Contract and

(2)   a supervisor of all the Contractor's activities on the Site, with full authority to receive instructions and other communications on behalf of the Contractor in all matters concerning the Contract.

The representative and the supervisor may, but need not, be the same person.

4.2.2   Matters of which the Contractor's representative or supervisor are aware [including communications and instructions] are presumed to be within the Contractor's knowledge.

4.2.3   If the Contractor's representative or supervisor are named in the Works Proposals, the Contractor shall appoint the individuals named. If not, or either of them is changed, the Contractor shall submit details of the proposed representative or supervisor to the

Employer's Representative. If the Contractor's representative or supervisor dies, or becomes incapable of performing their role, or is no longer available to the Contractor, the Contractor shall appoint a suitable replacement, having submitted details to the Employer's Representative. If the Employer's Representative so requires because of the misconduct, negligence or incompetence of either of them, the Contractor shall remove its representative or supervisor and appoint a suitable replacement, having submitted details to the Employer's Representative.

NOTE

This sub-clause deals with the Contractor's supervision. The Contractor must notify the Employer's Representative of the name of the Contractor's representative or supervisor before the start date. If named in the work proposals, they shall be the persons appointed unless a change is notified to the Employer's Representative. The Employer's Representative has the power to have the Contractor remove a Contractor's representative or supervisor arising from misconduct, negligence or incompetence. The Contractor shall comply with the Employer's Representative's requirement having submitted details to the Employer's Representative.

4.3   Employer's Representative

4.3.1   If the Employer's Representative is not named in the Schedule, part 1A, the Employer shall, promptly after the Contract Date, appoint, and notify the Contractor of the identity of, the Employer's Representative.

4.3.2   If there are limitations on the authority of the Employer's Representative to perform its functions or powers under the Contract, they are stated in the Contract. But any act or instruction of the Employer's Representative under the Contract shall have effect as if within the Employer's Representative's authority, and the Contractor need not inquire into whether the Employer has actually authorised it.

4.3.3   The Employer's Representative may delegate in writing to named representatives any functions or powers under the Contract and revoke any delegation. The appointment of such a representative shall not prevent the Employer's Representative from exercising directly any functions or powers. The Employer's Representative shall notify the Contractor and the Employer of any delegation, and the names of representatives, and of any subsequent changes, within 5 working days after the event in each case.

4.3.4   Any opinion, certificate, determination, assessment or objection of the Employer's Representative under the Contract may be revised in accordance with clause 13, except for decisions stated in the Contract to be conclusive [such as rejection of a Defect under subclause 8.5.4].

4.3.5   The Employer may replace the Employer's Representative at any time, notifying the Contractor of the replacement, and shall do so promptly if the position of Employer's Representative becomes vacant before the Defects Certificate (or alternatively the certificates required following termination) have been issued. Pending appointment of a replacement, the Employer shall carry out the functions and powers of the Employer's Representative.

4.4   Employer's Representative's Communications

4.4.1   The Employer's Representative may give the Contractor

(1)   instructions, which are either

(a)   directions in accordance with the Contract or

(b)   Change Orders and

(2)   objections, in accordance with sub-clause 4.7.

4.4.2 The Employer's Representative may give the Contractor or the Employer, or both

(1) opinions, assessments, determinations and certificates, in accordance with the Contract and

(2) other communications [including clarifications] in accordance with the Contract or the Employer's Representative considers appropriate.

NOTE

The Employer's Representative may give the Contractor instructions which can be either:

(i) Directions in accordance with the Contract; or

(ii) Change Orders.

The Employer's Representative may also object to any of the Contractor's proposals in accordance with sub-clause 4.7.

The Employer's Representative may also give opinions, assessments, determinations and certificates in accordance with the Contract and other communications, including clarifications, in accordance with the Contract or as the Employer's Representative considers appropriate.

Despite the apparent restrictions mentioned under the Schedule in Part 1A, the Employer's Representative has similar powers to both the engineer and architect under the IEI or GDLA forms of contracts. The Employer's Representative may issue instructions up to the issue of the Defects Certificate. The Employer's Representative may change the Work Requirements, impose, change or remove restrictions on the way the work is done and/or give instructions on defects.

Instructions are to be given to the Contractor when requested in the time required under sub-clause 4.11.

4.5   Instructions

4.5.1 The Employer's Representative may issue instructions to the Contractor on any matter connected with the Works [whether or not mentioned elsewhere in the Contract] at any time up to the date the Defects Certificate is issued. The Contractor shall comply with an instruction of the Employer's Representative.

4.5.2 If the Employer's Representative gives an instruction and calls it a direction, but the Contractor considers that it is a Change Order, the Contractor shall be entitled to give notice under sub-clause 10.3, and have the issue determined under clause 10. In addition to the requirements of sub-clause 10.3, the Contractor must give this notice before starting to implement the instruction, otherwise it will be taken to be a direction.

4.5.3 The Employer's Representative shall not give a Change Order concerning the Works or a Section after its Substantial Completion has been certified, except concerning Defects or work to be done after Substantial Completion.

4.5.4 The Employer's Representative shall give an instruction that is, in the Employer's Representative's opinion, necessary for the completion of the Works. If, in the Employer's Representative's opinion, it is physically impossible or contrary to Legal Requirements to complete the Works in accordance with the Works Requirements, the Employer's Representative shall give a Change Order. The Employer's Representative shall give an instruction required under this sub-clause 4.5.4 within the time required by sub-clause 4.11.

4.5.5 Instructions of the Employer's Representative shall be given in writing except when there is imminent danger to safety or health or of damage to property, in which case the Employer's Representative may give oral instructions, and shall confirm them in writing as soon as practicable.

NOTE

The Employer's Representative issues all instructions on any matter connected with the Works at any time up to the date the Defects Certificate is issued. The Contractor must comply with all instructions. There is no facility for the Contractor to confirm or to work on verbal instructions, unless on matters of health and safety.

Sub-clause 4.5.2 provides that if the Employer's Representative issues a direction which the Contractor considers to be a "change order" then the Contractor can give notice under clause 10.3 and have the matter determined under clause 10. The Contractor must give this notice before starting to implement the instruction, otherwise it will be taken to be a direction. The Employer's Representative will make a determination under sub-clause 10.5. The Contractor, if dissatisfied with the Employer's Representative's determination, can refer the matter to conciliation.

All directions should be reviewed to establish if it is a change order. In the event of a change order being issued then it is a "Delay and Compensation Event" under Item 1 of Section K of the Schedule, Part 1.

4.6   Works Proposals

4.6.1   The Contractor shall ensure that all Works Proposals comply with the Works Requirements.

4.6.2   If any Works Proposals do not comply with the Contract or the Works Requirements or Legal Requirements or are physically impossible to comply with, the Contractor shall propose a change to the Works Proposals as necessary. [There shall be no extension of time or adjustment to the Contract Sum for this.] If the Works Proposals need to be changed because of a change to the Works Requirements, the Contractor shall propose a change. The Contractor shall submit any change to the Works Proposals to the Employer's Representative.

NOTE

If any works proposals do not comply with the Contract or the initial works requirements or are physically impossible to comply with, the Contractor shall propose a change to the works proposals as necessary. There shall be no extension of time or adjustment to the contract sum for this.

Condition 4.6.2 states that: "[i]f the Works Proposals need to be changed because of a change to the Works Requirements, the Contractor shall propose a change. The Contractor shall submit any change to the Works Proposals to the Employer's Representative." This proposal comes under Item 1 of Section K of the Schedule and is a "Delay Event" and a "Compensation Event".

Condition 4.6.1 requires the Contractor to provide a statement of the proposed action and all supporting information to the Employer's Representative.

4.7   Required Contractor Submissions

Unless the Works Requirements say that a different procedure is to apply, whenever the Contract requires that a document or proposed course of action be submitted to the Employer's Representative, the following shall apply:

4.7.1   The Contractor shall give the document or a statement of the proposed action and all necessary supporting information to the Employer's Representative.

4.7.2   The Employer's Representative may [but is not bound to] make a written objection to a Contractor's submission, giving reasons.

4.7.3   The Employer's Representative may request additional information.

4.7.4 The Employer's Representative's period for objection is 10 working days from when the Employer's Representative has received from the Contractor enough information to make a purposeful review of the matter submitted should it wish to make one.

4.7.5 The Contractor shall apply in writing for any reduction of the period that it considers desirable in the interests of the Works, which the Employer's Representative may agree if it thinks fit.

4.7.6 The Employer's Representative may alter or withdraw an objection.

4.7.7 The Contractor shall not implement any submission before the period has ended, or contrary to any outstanding objection given within the period.

4.7.8 The Contractor shall make a new submission to meet any objection given within the period.

4.7.9 The Contractor shall also make new submissions as necessary to perform its duties under the Contract [whether or not it has received any objection], and in particular so that its submitted programme shows actual and current planned progress.

4.7.10 The Employer's Representative may object on the grounds that to proceed according to the submission

(1) would not comply with the Contract or

(2) would have an adverse effect on the Employer or the public interest or

(3) would impose an obligation on the Employer that the Contract does not require the Employer to bear or

(4) would be contrary to a Legal Requirement or

(5) would have an adverse effect on the Contractor's ability to comply with the Contract or any other ground stated in the Contract.

4.7.11 Neither the Employer's Representative's rights to object, nor objections or their absence, reduce any of the Employer's Representative's other powers, or reduce any of the Contractor's responsibilities.

NOTE

The contract may require the Contractor to provide a document(s) or a proposed course of action to the Employer's Representative. If required, the Contractor shall provide a statement of the proposed action and all supporting information to the Employer's Representative. The Employer's Representative may object to the submission giving reasons. The Employer's Representative may request additional information. The Employer's Representative has 10 working days from when Contractor has provided *enough* information to object to the submission. How the words "enough information" are satisfied is a matter for the Employer's Representative. The Contractor can request a reduction in the time for review and the Employer's Representative may or may not agree as he thinks fit. New submissions may be necessary from the Contractor and the Contractor is obliged to produce these documents. In planning the programme such time periods must be allowed by the Contractor for such approvals and the timing for submissions and approvals needs to be identified clearly on the current programme.

4.8   (sub-clause not used)

4.9   Programme

4.9.1 Before the Starting Date, the Contractor shall submit to the Employer's Representative a detailed programme. If there is a programme in the Works Proposals that complies with the Contract, the Contractor shall submit that programme, with any required additional information [such as the actual programmed dates]. The programme shall be of a quality that will permit effective monitoring of the Works and shall include details of when the Contractor will require any instructions, Works Items or other things to be given by the Employer, or anything else the Contract requires the Employer, the Employer's Representative or others to give the Contractor.

4.9.2 The Contractor's programme shall allow reasonable periods of time for the Employer and the Employer's Personnel to comply with their obligations under the Contract.

4.9.3 If the Contractor's programme most recently submitted to the Employer's Representative does not correspond with actual or reasonably projected progress or the Contractor's obligations, the Contractor shall, if so directed by the Employer's Representative, submit to the Employer's Representative a revised programme that complies with this sub-clause and the other provisions of the Contract, showing actual progress and progress projected by the Contractor. If the Contractor asserts that it is not possible to reach Substantial Completion of the Works or a Section by its Date for Substantial Completion, the revised programme shall show Substantial Completion by the earliest possible date. [Neither the programme nor its review will limit the Contractor's responsibility or liability for the delay.] If the Contractor fails to submit the revised programme within 15 working days of a request from the Employer's Representative, the Employer shall be entitled to withhold from the Contractor 15% of any payment to be made to the Contractor until the revised programme is submitted.

> **NOTE**
>
> The programme will be a key document under this Contract. Programme computer software will be a necessary requirement. The programme shall include details of when the Contractor will require any instructions, works items or other things to be given by the Employer, or anything else the contract requires the Employer, the Employer's Representative or others to give the Contractor. The programme will be a fundamental monitoring tool of the progress of the works. The programme will be the primary document for the assessment of entitlements arising from delay and compensation events.
>
> Contractors should note that if the Contractor fails to provide a revised programme within 15 working days of a request from the Employer's Representative, then the Employer may withhold 15 percent of the value of any payment due to the Contractor until the new programme is provided.

4.10 Progress Reports

The Contractor shall give the Employer's Representative monthly progress reports from the Starting Date until the Contractor has completed all work outstanding on Substantial Completion of the Works. The first report shall cover the period from the Starting Date up to the end of the month in which it occurs, and each subsequent report shall cover one month. The Contractor shall give each progress report within 7 days after the end of the month it relates to. Each progress report shall be in a form agreed by the Employer's Representative and shall include detailed description of progress of each stage of the Works against the Contractor's current programme and anything else relevant to a progress report that the Employer's Representative directs.

> **NOTE**
>
> Progress reports are, like the programme, are an essential element for the management of the contract and clause 4.10 sets out the requirements.

4.11 Notice and Time for Employer's Obligations

4.11.1 The Contractor shall give the Employer's Representative at least 10 working days advance notice of the date by which the Contractor requires any instructions that the Employer's Representative is to give, or Works Items or other things that the Employer is to give.

4.11.2 The latest date for the Employer's Representative to give required instructions, or the Employer to give the Contractor any required Works Item or other thing, shall be the latest of the following:

(1) the date stated in the Contract, if any

(2) the date shown in the Contractor's current programme

(3) the date for which the Contractor first notifies the Employer's Representative under this sub-clause that it is required

(4) the date the Contractor requires the instruction, Works Item or other thing in accordance with its actual progress.

> **NOTE**
>
> The Contractor must provide 10 working days advance notice of the date by which instructions are required from the Employer's Representative for work items or other things that the Employer is to provide. This information can be developed when producing the programme. A separate letter with a request for information should also be sent to the Employer's Representative. Any failure by the Employer's Representative to provide the requested information on time may entitle the Contractor to an extension of time and costs in accordance with Item 7 of Section K of Part 1 of the Schedule.

4.12   Documents

The Contractor shall keep on the Site all of the following:

(1) a full up-to-date set of the Contract documents (but the Pricing Document may be unpriced), instructions of the Employer's Representative, and Contractor's Documents

(2) a log of all instructions and Contractor's Documents showing dates of issue for each and any subsequent revisions

(3) if requested by the Employer's Representative, all publications named in the Contract and the Contractor's Documents.

The Employer's Representative, and any person authorised by the Employer's Representative, shall have a right of access to these at all reasonable times.

> **NOTE**
>
> The Contractor is obliged to keep a copy of all documents, including documents referred to in the Contract, with the exception of the Contractor's prices. All documents can be accessed by the Employer's Representative or any person authorized by the Employer's Representative.

4.13   Contractor's Management

4.13.1 The Contractor's business includes expertise and experience in construction management.

4.13.2 The Works Proposals include details of the Contractor's initial management arrangements for performing its Contract responsibilities.

4.13.3 The Contractor shall implement the arrangements, and shall add to and otherwise change them, as desirable for its efficient performance.

4.13.4 The arrangements shall include systems, methods, planning and other preparations for providing personnel and resources, programming, recording, consultation, co-ordination, and co-operation, and for flexibility, as referred to in the Contract.

4.13.5 The Contractor shall keep the Employer's Representative fully informed about its current arrangements, in advance, and about their implementation.

4.13.6 The Contractor shall give the Employer's Representative all information, documents and records in the possession of, or available to, the Contractor or the Contractor's Personnel, that the Employer's Representative requires to perform its functions and powers under the Contract.

> **NOTE**
>
> The Contractor must keep the Employer's Representative fully informed about all arrangements for the works and provide the Employer's Representative with all the documents that he may need to carry out his function under the contract.

4.14 Communications

4.14.1 The parties intend all communications between them to be interpreted purposefully, having regard to the Contract's purposes.

4.14.2 Whenever any communication [including a notice, decision, objection, approval, certificate, determination, instruction or request] is to be given under the Contract it shall, unless the Contract provides otherwise, be in English, in writing and delivered as follows:

(1) for notices under clause 12 or clause 13, delivered by hand or sent by pre-paid registered post to the address for those notices in the Schedule, part 1A, as updated by the relevant party

(2) for other communications, delivered by hand or sent by pre-paid post, fax or email according to the particulars for other communications in the Schedule, part 1A, as updated by the relevant party.

4.14.3 Communications by pre-paid registered post are presumed to have been received at 10:00 a.m. two working days after posting. Fax and email communications are presumed to have been received when receipt is electronically recorded.

> **NOTE**
>
> All communications under the contract must be in writing and delivered as follows:
>
> (i) Clause 12 (Termination) and 13 (Disputes) must be delivered/sent by registered post to the address given in Part 1A of the Schedule.
>
> (ii) Other communications must be delivered, posted, faxed or e-mailed to the relevant party according to the details in Part 1A of the Schedule.
>
> Postal communications are presumed delivered at 10.00 hours, two working days after posting. This is important for ensuring compliance with the strict timetables set down in clauses 9 (Time and Completion) and 10 (Claims and Adjustments). Faxes or e-mails are presumed received when receipt is electronically recorded.

4.15 Meetings

4.15.1 The Contractor's representative and the Employer's Representative shall attend regular meetings scheduled by the Employer's Representative and any special meeting called by either of them to discuss a particular issue identified when calling the meeting. The Employer's Representative may invite other Employer's Personnel and the Contractor may invite Contractor's Personnel to attend meetings. The Contractor shall arrange for the attendance at a meeting of any Contractor's Personnel requested by the Employer's Representative. The time and place of meetings shall be set by the Employer's Representative, after consulting the Contractor, acting reasonably.

4.15.2 Within 5 working days after each meeting the Employer's Representative shall issue minutes of the meeting to the Employer and the Contractor. The Contractor shall notify the

Employer's Representative of any objection to the minutes within 5 working days of receiving them, otherwise, unless clearly wrong, they shall be considered correct.

> **NOTE**
>
> Regular meetings shall take place between the Contractor and the Employer's Representative. Special meetings may be called and Employer's Personnel may be requested to attend. The Employer's Representative will issue the minutes within five working days of the meeting. The Contractor then has five working days to object to any minute, and otherwise unless clearly wrong, the minutes are considered correct.

4.16   Confidentiality and Secrecy

4.16.1   The Contractor shall [and shall ensure that the Contractor's Personnel shall] keep confidential:

(1)   official information as defined in the Official Secrets Act 1963 and

(2)   other information stated in the Works Requirements to be confidential or secret, or that the Employer or the Employer's Representative notifies the Contractor is confidential or secret.

4.16.2   The Employer shall keep confidential the Contractor's rates and prices in the Pricing Document or provided in accordance with the Contract, and any records given by the Contractor under the Contract that the Contractor notifies the Employer's Representative are confidential.

4.16.3   This sub-clause 4.16 shall not prevent disclosure of information, to the extent permitted by Law

(1)   to the Contractor's Personnel, the Employer's Personnel or other professional advisors to the Contractor or Employer, who have first entered an undertaking in the terms of this sub-clause 4.16, to the extent necessary for the execution of the Works or to enforce the Contract or

(2)   when required by Law or order of a court or, in the case of disclosure by the Employer, for governmental, parliamentary, statutory, administrative, fiscal or judicial purposes, or the publication of an award notice or

(3)   that has, except as a result of breach of confidentiality, become available or generally known to the public at the time of the disclosure.

4.16.4   The Contractor's obligations under this sub-clause 4.16 shall be perpetual. The Employer's obligations under this sub-clause shall expire when the commercial sensitivity of the relevant information has ceased, in any event 5 years after the information was given.

> **NOTE**
>
> This is the confidentiality clause. Details of the Contractor's rates and work proposals are to be kept confidential by the Employer and the Employer's Representative. This sub-clause shall not prevent disclosure permitted by law, to enable Contractor to complete the contract. The Contractor's obligation is perpetual. The Employer's obligation is limited to five years.

4.17   Contractor's Things Not to Be Removed

The Contractor shall submit details to the Employer's Representative before removing any Contractor's Things from the Site before the Employer's Representative issues a certificate of Substantial Completion of the Works or relevant Section.

NOTE

The Contractor must inform the Employer's Representative before he removes any of the Contractor's "things" from site before the Employer's Representative issues a Certificate of Substantial Completion. "Contractor's things" are equipment, facilities and other things the Contractor uses to execute the works, except works items. "Works items" means a part of the works or anything the Contractor intends will become part of the works and temporary works for the works.

4.18   Contractor's Documents

All Contractor's Documents shall be in English, except when the Works Requirements or the Law specify another language.

GENERAL NOTE ON SECTION

Clause 4 sets out the manner in which this Contract will be managed and administered. The Contractor must appreciate the substantial management burden imposed on him by this contract. Effective management and administration is essential and must be compliant with the requirements expressed under clause 4.

5   CONTRACTOR'S PERSONNEL

5.1   Contractor's Personnel to Carry Out Contractor's Obligations

The Contractor is liable for the acts and omissions of Contractor's Personnel [including Specialists and any design they do] as if they were the Contractor's acts and omissions.

5.2   Qualifications and Competence

The Contractor shall ensure that the Contractor's Personnel are suitably qualified and experienced and are competent to carry out their respective tasks.

5.3   Pay and Conditions of Employment

5.3.1   The Contractor shall prominently exhibit copies of this sub-clause 5.3 for the information of persons at the Site. In this sub-clause 5.3 **work person** means an individual employed by, or otherwise working for, the Contractor or the Contractor's Personnel on or adjacent to the Site.

5.3.2   The Contractor shall ensure that the rates of pay and the conditions of employment [including in relation to pension contributions] of each work person comply with all applicable Law, and that those rates and conditions are no less favourable than those for the relevant category of work person in any employment agreements registered under the Industrial Relations Acts 1946 to 2004. The obligations in this sub-clause 5.3 apply regardless of what rates the Contractor has tendered for adjustments to the Contract Sum.

5.3.3   The Contractor shall in respect of

(i)   work persons employed by, or otherwise working for, the Contractor and

(ii)   all other work persons, ensure that their employers, or the persons for whom they are working,

do all of the following:

(1)   pay all wages and other money due to each work person

(2)   ensure that work persons' wages are paid in accordance with the Payment of Wages Act 1991 and are never more than 1 month in arrears or unpaid

(3)   pay all pension contributions and other amounts due to be paid on behalf of each work person

(4)   make all deductions from payments to work persons required by Law, and pay them on as required by Law

(5)   keep proper records [including time sheets, wage books and copies of pay slips] showing the wages and other sums paid to and the time worked by each work person, deductions from each work person's pay and their disposition, and pension and other contributions made in respect of each work person, and produce these records for inspection and copying by any persons authorised by the Employer, whenever required by the Employer

(6)   produce any other records relating to the rates of pay, pension and other contributions, deductions from pay and their disposition, conditions of employment of work persons, rest periods, and annual leave for inspection and copying by any persons authorised by the Employer, whenever required by the Employer

(7)   respect the right under law of work persons to be members of trade unions

(8)   observe, in relation to the employment of work persons on the Site, the Safety, Health and Welfare at Work Act, 2005 and all employment law including the Employment Equality Act 1998, the Industrial Relations Acts 1946 to 2004, the National Minimum Wage Act 2000, and regulations, codes of practice, legally binding determinations of the Labour Court and registered employment agreements under those laws.

5.3.3A

(1)   Sub-clause 5.3.3A(2) shall only be included in the Contract if the Schedule, part 1J says so, and if not, neither sub-clause 5.3.3A(2) nor its omission shall be taken into account.

(2)   The Employer shall be entitled to make random checks requiring production of records under sub-clauses 5.3.3(5) and (6).

5.3.4   If the Employer so requests, the Contractor shall, within 5 working days after the receipt of the request, give to the Employer a statement showing the amount of wages and other payments due at the date of the request to and in respect of each work person, or, in respect of work persons not employed by or otherwise working for the Contractor, ensure that their employer or the person for whom they are working does the same.

5.3.5   The Employer may seek information under sub-clause 5.3.3 only for the purpose of ensuring the obligations referred to in this sub-clause 5.3 to work persons have been properly discharged. All information given under sub-clause 5.3.3 shall be returned to the person providing them or destroyed if the Employer is satisfied that the relevant employer has complied with legal obligations to work persons.

5.3.6   If the Contractor has not complied with this sub-clause 5.3, the Employer shall [without limiting its other rights or remedies] be entitled to estimate the amount that should have been paid to work persons and contributions that should have been made on their behalf, and the Employer may deduct the estimated amount from any payment due to the Contractor, until the Employer is satisfied that all proper amounts have been paid.

5.3.7   The Contractor shall give the Employer's Representative with each interim statement under sub-clause 11.1 a certificate in the form in the Works Requirements, that, in respect of the work to which the interim certificate relates, the Contractor has complied in full with this sub-clause 5.3.

5.3.8   If the Contractor does not comply with this sub-clause 5.3, it shall pay to the Employer any costs the Employer incurs in investigating and dealing with the non-compliance.

NOTE

The Contractor shall ensure that the rates of pay and conditions of employment of each work person comply with applicable law and are no less favourable than those for the relevant category of work person in any employment agreement registered under the Industrial Relations Acts 1946–2004. The Contractor is also responsible for the compliance of sub-contractors, including labour hire, with this condition. The Contractor is responsible for the enforcement of these requirements and any breach can be grounds for termination.

To confirm the Contractor's compliance with condition 5.3, condition 5.3.7 requires the Contractor to provide the Employer's Representative with a certificate (in the form in the works requirements) that the Contractor has complied in full with sub-clause 5.3. This certificate has to be submitted with each interim statement submitted by the Contractor under sub-clause 11.1 (Interim Payment); otherwise there will be no payment for the relevant work item until the certificate is given.

5.4   Subcontractors and Specialists

5.4.1   The Contractor shall not subcontract all of the Works to one or more Subcontractors. If the Contractor intends to subcontract part of the Works, other than when the Subcontractor and its scope are set out in the Contract, or the Contract provides other procedures, the Contractor shall first submit details to the Employer's Representative of the proposed Subcontractor and its proposed scope of work. The Contractor shall also submit details to the Employer's Representative of any proposed Specialist, other than one named in the Contract or when the Contract provides other procedures.

NOTE

The Contract allows for "named Sub-Contractors" (Specialists). All Sub-Contractors will be engaged on a domestic basis. The Contractor has to obtain the acceptance of the Employer's Representative to any proposed Specialist.

5.4.2   If Specialists or other Contractor's Personnel are named in the Contract, the Contractor shall ensure that they are engaged for and perform the work for which they are named.

NOTE

If the Specialist or other Contractor's personnel are named in the Employer's Work Requirements the Contractor shall ensure that they are engaged for the works set out and named in the Contract.

The following pre-tender procedures will apply:

* The tender for the specialist work will be completed before the competition for the main Contract;

* The name of the Specialist, the sub-contract price and the sub-contract agreement will be included in the works requirements issued to tender.

The Employer should obtain an undertaking from the Specialist that he will enter into a sub-contract with the Contractor on terms and obligations that apply under the main Contract. There is no right of objection from the Contractor as the Specialist is named in the tender document which he cannot alter and is therefore part of his bid.

5.4.3   If the Works Requirements name a Specialist whose contract with the Employer is to be novated to the Contractor, and include a copy of that contract, the Contractor shall accept the novation, and the parties shall, at the same time as entering the Agreement, enter the novation agreement in the Works Requirements.

NOTE

If the work requirements name a Specialist whose contract is to be novated to the Contractor and includes a copy of the contract, the Contractor shall accept the novation and execute the novation agreement at the same time as the main contract is executed. The process at tender stage is similar to 5.4.2 above. The Employer's Representative may not instruct the Contractor to enter into a sub-contract with the Specialist selected by the Employer's Representative unless that Specialist was named in the contract.

5.4.4   The Employer's Representative may not instruct the Contractor to enter a contract with a particular Specialist selected by the Employer's Representative unless the Specialist is named in the Contract.

5.4.5   The Contractor shall fully comply with its obligations under any contract with a Specialist and shall not terminate, allow to be terminated or accept a repudiation of such a contract without first submitting details to the Employer's Representative, except when an insolvency event, as set out in sub-clause 12.1, occurs in respect of the Specialist, or the Specialist has committed a serious breach of Law concerning safety, or the Specialist has failed to put or keep in effect insurance as required by the Specialist's contract. On any termination, the

Contractor shall replace the Specialist, having submitted details of the replacement to the Employer's Representative.

NOTE

The Contractor shall comply fully with the sub-contract with the Specialist and cannot terminate without notifying the Employer's Representative except for insolvency or a serious breach of the law in relation to safety or a failure to comply with insurance requirements. On any terminations the Contractor shall organise a replacement with a specialist approved by the Employer's Representative.

5.4.6 In addition to the reasons in sub-clause 4.7, the Employer's Representative may object to the proposed replacement of Contractor's Personnel because the proposed replacement does not have at least the level of experience, qualifications, competence, technical capacity, and financial standing of the person being replaced.

5.5 Collateral Warranties

If the Schedule, part 1F, states that a collateral warranty is required from any Specialist, before the date stated in the Schedule, the Contractor shall give the Employer a collateral warranty in the form included in the Works Requirements, or if there is none, a form approved by the Employer, executed by the Specialist and the Contractor. The minimum indemnity limit and maximum excess of professional indemnity insurance required of the Specialist shall be as stated in the Schedule, part 1F.

NOTE

This clause deals with collateral warranties. Note should be taken of the critical dates and the amounts that may be withheld from payments due to the Contractor for failure to meet those dates.

5.6 Removal of Work Persons

The Contractor shall remove from the Site any Contractor's Personnel that the Employer's Representative directs, because of the Contractor's Personnel's negligence or incompetence, or on the basis that the Contractor's Personnel's presence on the Site is not conducive to safety, health or good order.

GENERAL NOTES ON SECTION

This clause sets out that the Contractor is liable for the acts and omissions of Contractor's Personnel (including Specialists and any design they do) as if they were the Contractor's acts and omissions.

This clause deals with the warranty with regard to experience and competence. It also introduces the strict requirements of Pay and Conditions of Employment. The Contractor's obligation to ensure compliance with the provisions extends to every work person engaged on or adjacent to the site for the Contractor or his Sub-Contractors and other persons assisting the Contractor to perform the contract.

The Contract allows for the novation of contracts between the Employer and a Specialist to the Contractor. In this event the Contractor assumes the role and responsibilities of the Employer. Should a specialist be novated to the Contractor in this manner, the Contractor shall have no right to object to the appointment of the specialist.

6 PROPERTY

6.1 Ownership of Works Items

It is agreed, and the Contractor shall ensure, that each Works Item shall become the property of the Employer on the earliest of the following:

    (1)   when it is delivered to the Site, if owned by the Contractor

    (2)   when it is incorporated in the Works

    (3)   when any payment for the Works Item is made by the Employer to the Contractor.

NOTE

This sub-clause deals with ownership of work items and is particularly relevant to situations of insolvency. The Contractor is to ensure property passes to Employer on the earliest of the following: when it is delivered to the site if owned by the Contractor; when it is incorporated into the works; or, when any payment for the works item is made by the Employer. "Work items" means a part of the works, or anything that the Contractor intends will become part of the works and temporary works for the works.

6.2 Infringement of Property Rights

6.2.1   The Contractor shall indemnify the Employer against any liability resulting from any of the following infringing the property [including intellectual property] rights of any person:

    (1)   the Contractor's performance or non-performance of this Contract, unless the liability is covered by the Employer's indemnity in this sub-clause

    (2)   use of Works Items, Contractor's Things, or Contractor's Documents by

        (a)   the Contractor or Contractor's Personnel or

        (b)   the Employer or any other person to complete the Works following termination of the Contractor's obligation to complete the Works

    (3)   use by the Employer of the Works, Works Items, or the Contractor's Documents for the purpose for which they were given.

6.2.2   The Employer shall indemnify the Contractor against any liability resulting from any of the following infringing the property [including intellectual property] rights of any person:

    (1)   the unavoidable use by the Contractor, in accordance with the Contract, of the Works Requirements or Works Items or other things provided by the Employer

    (2)   the use or occupation by the Works of the parts of the Site described in the Works Requirements as lands made available by the Employer for the Works, when that is the unavoidable result of performing the Contract.

NOTE

Sub-clause 6.2 deals with indemnifying both the Employer and the Contractor from infringement of property rights, including intellectual rights.

6.3 Works Requirements

The Works Requirements shall remain the property of the Employer and the Contractor shall not use them [and shall ensure that the Contractor's Personnel do not use them] for any purpose other than to perform the Contract or to prosecute or defend a dispute under the Contract.

6.4 Rights in Contractor's Documents

6.4.1 The Employer may use, copy, modify, adapt and translate for any purpose in connection with the Works [including to construct, maintain, extend, use, operate, let, sell, promote, advertise, reinstate and repair the Works] the Contractor's Documents that are given, or, according to the Contract, must be given, to the Employer and the Works Proposals.

6.4.2 Where the Schedule, part 1O, so states, all copyright and other rights in the Contractor's Documents that are prepared for the Works and are given, or according to the Contract, must be given, to the Employer and the Works Proposals transfers to the Employer when the Employer receives them.

6.4.3 The Contractor shall ensure that the Employer obtains the rights and interests described in this sub-clause 6.4.

6.4.4 The Contractor has no liability for the use of the Contractor's Documents for any purpose other than that for which they were given to the Employer.

NOTE

Sub-clause 6.4 deals with the property and rights in the Contractor's documents, which the Employer has the right to use, copy, modify, adopt or translate for any purpose in connection with the works. Part 1O of the Schedule may state that handover of copyright to the Employer and the Contractor shall ensure that all those rights can be transferred, including copyright to documents provided by Contractor's personnel. The Contractor is not liable for the use of the Contractor's documents for any purpose other than that for which they were provided to the Employer.

GENERAL NOTES ON SECTION

This clause deals with property rights associated with the works. The Employer is concerned with ensuring that he will receive clear title to anything which will be incorporated into his building and, in this regard, the Contractor is required to obtain clear title to items to be incorporated into the works.

This clause provides that the Employer retains ownership of the Works requirements, whilst he must *obtain* ownership of the Contractor's Documents should the Employer wish to exercise this option.

7 THE SITE

7.1 Lands Made Available for the Works

7.1.1 The Employer shall allow the Contractor to occupy and use each part of the Site described in the Works Requirements as lands made available by the Employer for the Works from a date on or before the latest of the following:

    (1)   the Starting Date

    (2)   the day after the Contractor has done what sub-clause 9.1 requires the Contractor to do before the Starting Date

    (3)   the date stated in the Works Requirements, if any

    (4)   the day after the Contractor has submitted its programme according to sub-clause 4.9

    (5)   the date stated for work to start on the part of the Site in the Contractor's current programme

    (6)   the date the Contractor actually requires the part in accordance with its actual progress.

7.1.2 The Contractor's right to occupy and use the Site shall be subject to any limitations in the Works Requirements.

> **NOTE**
>
> The possession and access to the site will be subject to limitations as expressed in the work requirements.

7.1.3 The Contractor shall not be entitled to exclusive possession of the Site or any part of it and shall facilitate any occupation and use of the Site by the Employer and others stated in the Works Requirements. The Contractor's right to occupy and use the Site shall be solely for the purpose of performing the Contract.

7.1.4 The Contractor's right to occupy and use the Site shall end when the Employer's Representative certifies the Works or the relevant Section as Substantially Complete. After then the Employer shall allow the Contractor access to comply with sub-clause 8.6.1.

7.1.5 The Contractor's right to occupy and use the Site shall end if the Contractor's obligation to complete the Works is terminated.

> **NOTE**
>
> The Employer shall allow access to the site on or before the latest of the following dates:
>
>   (i)   The starting date – which is the date the Contractor proposes to start executing the works on site, as notified by the Contractor to the Employer's Representative.
>
>   (ii)   The day after the Contractor has done what sub-clause 9.1 (Starting Date) requires the Contractor to do before the starting date. This includes to:
>
>   (a)   Execute the agreement;
>
>   (b)   Provide the performance bond;
>
>   (c)   Provide the parent company guarantee;
>
>   (d)   If it is required by the Contract execute the appointment of the Contractor as Project Supervisor;
>
>   (e)   Provide evidence that all insurances are in place;

       (f)   Provide any Collateral Warranties (these may be supplied later with the agreement of the Employer's Representative).

  (iii) The date stated in the works requirement.

  (iv) The day after the Contractor has submitted its programme in accordance with sub-clause 4.9.

  (v) The day stated for work to start on part of the site in the Contractor's current programme.

  (vi) The date the Contractor actually requires the part in accordance with its actual programme.

The Contractor must insure all the Contract requirements are in place in advance of the starting date, otherwise the Employer does not have to give access to the site.

By sub-clause 7.1.3 the Contractor is not entitled to exclusive possession of the site.

7.2   Trespassers

After the Employer has allowed the Contractor to occupy and use the Site, the Contractor shall be responsible for activities of trespassers, protesters and others, that are not Employer's Personnel, on the Site, and the Employer shall have no responsibility to the Contractor for their activities or presence.

NOTE

The Contractor is responsible for trespassers and the Employer shall have no responsibility to the Contractor for their activities or presence. The Contractor will have to study the Work Requirements to establish if any parts of the site or facilities have to be operated and maintained during the course of the Works. Any costs involved will have to be built into the tender. In the event that facilities have to be operated the full extent of such should be determined as it could have serious implications on cost and resources.

7.3   Contractor Responsible for All Site Operations

The Contractor shall be responsible for all operations on the Site connected with the execution of the Works.

7.4   Services for Employer's Facilities

The Contractor shall operate and maintain parts of the Site and facilities of the Employer if the Works Requirements so require.

NOTE

The extent of what is meant by "operate and maintain" is new and would need to be carefully checked from the work requirements. Operate is not usually a "Contractor" function so this could be a serious resource and cost issue.

7.5   Security and Safety of the Site and Nuisance

7.5.1   From and including the Starting Date until the Employer's Representative certifies the Works or the relevant Section as Substantially Complete, the Contractor shall do all of the following [without limiting other obligations]:

  (1) be responsible for securing the Site and for keeping off the Site persons other than any of the following:

    (i) the Contractor's Personnel and the Employer's Personnel

    (ii) any other person notified to the Contractor by the Employer or the Employer's Representative as authorised to enter the Site

      (iii)   persons exercising public access to any roads, footpaths and areas on the Site

      (iv)   persons having a right to enter the Site under Legal Requirements

  (2) keep the Site in good order and free from unnecessary obstructions

  (3) take all necessary steps to secure the safety of all persons entitled to be on the Site and to protect users, owners and occupiers of land adjacent to the Site from hazards and interference arising from the Works [including providing any required fences, lighting, guarding, watching, roads and footpaths]

  (4) take all necessary steps to ensure that the Contractor, the Contractor's Personnel and the execution of the Works do not do any of the following:

      (i)   unnecessarily cause a nuisance or inconvenience to the public or any user, owner or occupier of any land, road or footpath on or adjacent to the Site

      (ii)   unnecessarily interfere with the use of any such land, road or footpath.

7.5.2   The Employer shall ensure that Employer's Personnel on the Site comply with the Contractor's reasonable safety rules that have been notified to them by the Contractor.

> **NOTE**
>
> This sub-clause deals with security and safety of site and nuisance, which are normal Contractor responsibilities. The Contractor has to permit the public to continue to exercise their right of public access to roads, footpaths and areas on the site.

7.6   Other Contractors

Where so stated in the Works Requirements, the Employer may arrange for work to be executed on the Site by Employer's Personnel. The Contractor shall co-operate with such Employer's Personnel and shall as far as practicable co-ordinate their activities with the execution of the Works.

> **NOTE**
>
> The Contractor has to allow access to the Employer's Personnel which are the Employer's Representative, the Employer's Employees, agents and consultants, other Contractors of the Employer working on the site when acting within the scope of their contracts with the Employer, and, finally, anyone else the Employer's Representative advises the Contractor is an Employer's Personnel.

7.7   Setting Out the Works

The Contractor shall set out the Works by reference to the points, lines and levels of reference in the Works Requirements. The Contractor shall be responsible for the correct positioning of all parts of the Works and shall rectify any errors in the positions, levels, dimensions or alignment of the Works. Before setting out the Works the Contractor shall make all reasonable efforts to verify the accuracy of the setting out information in the Works Requirements.

> **NOTE**
>
> The Contractor is responsible for setting out the works correctly by reference to the information provided in the works requirements. In the event that any changes to the information provided causes a change to the work requirements then it should be recorded by the Contractor, notified to the Employer's Representative and a "change order" be should be requested.

7.8   Archaeological Objects and Human Remains

If any fossils, coins, antiquities, monuments or other items of value or of archaeological or geological interest or human remains are discovered on or adjacent to the Site, the Contractor shall not disturb them, but shall take all necessary steps to preserve them, and shall promptly notify the Employer's Representative [and comply with any instructions]. As between the parties, these items shall be the Employer's property.

> **NOTE**
>
> This clause sets out the steps the Contractor has to take in the event of archaeological objects or human remains been encountered on site. Item 18 of Section K of the Schedule, Part 1, provides for a delay and compensation event in these circumstances.

7.9   Access and Facilities

7.9.1   The Contractor [and not the Employer] shall be responsible for the suitability and availability of access routes to and within the Site, and any required maintenance or upgrading of them, and any charges for use of them.

7.9.2   The Contractor shall also be responsible for obtaining any additional facilities, and for providing all power, water and other services it requires to perform the Contract.

> **NOTE**
>
> The Contractor is responsible for the suitability and availability of access routes to the site, within the site, including upgrading, maintenance and paying any charges arising.

7.10   (sub-clause not used)

7.11   (sub-clause not used)

7.12   Charges

The Contractor shall pay any charges provided for in the Works Requirements for occupation of the Site or any part of it or other place, or in respect of operation or maintenance of Employer's facilities, or in respect of services, or otherwise. [The Employer may deduct the amount of charges from payments to the Contractor. Payment of charges does not excuse the Contractor from any of its obligations].

> **GENERAL NOTES ON SECTION**
>
> This clause sets out the obligations of the Parties in relation to delivery and occupation of the Site. The Employer is required to deliver the site, or any part of it, to the Contractor by, at the latest, the date upon which the Contractor actually requires the part of the site in accordance with actual progress. The Contractor will not obtain exclusive possession of the site or any part of it. This clause places the responsibility for trespassers with the Contractor. The only people who will be contractually compelled to abide by the Contractor's safety rules will be the Employer's and Contractor's personnel.
>
> The Contractor, from the starting date, becomes entirely responsible for all operations on the site (Clause 7.5.1), and for safety and security.
>
> The Contractor is responsible for setting out in accordance with the works requirements.

8   QUALITY, TESTING AND DEFECTS

8.1   Standards of Workmanship and Works Items

The Contractor shall ensure all of the following:

(1) that the Works are executed and completed

(i) in accordance with all the requirements in, and reasonably inferred from, the Contract [including, where so required by the Contract, in accordance with Contractor's Documents that have been submitted to the Employer's Representative] and

(ii) in a proper and workmanlike manner and using good practice

(2) that all Works Items [whether or not the Contractor is required to select them]

(i) comply with the Contract and the Legal Requirements and

(ii) are of good quality and, unless the Contract provides otherwise, new

(3) that all materials and goods that are Works Items [whether or not the Contractor is required to select them] are fit for the purpose for which they are normally used

(4) that all Works Items selected or designed by the Contractor [including by any Specialist] are fit for their intended purpose in the Works.

> **NOTE**
>
> All materials and goods are to be new and of good quality unless otherwise provided in the work requirements.

8.2   Quality Assurance

The Contractor shall establish and implement quality assurance procedures as required by the Works Requirements, including procedures for establishing quality assurance systems for itself and Subcontractors. The quality assurance procedures shall be reflected in appropriate quality plans submitted to the Employer's Representative. The Contractor shall give the Employer's Representative copies of all reports prepared in accordance with the Contractor's quality assurance procedures. The Employer's Representative may monitor, spot check and audit the Contractor's quality assurance procedures.

> **NOTE**
>
> Sub-clause 8.2 deals with the expected quality assurance procedures that the Contractor shall establish. The Employer's Representative is entitled to a copy of the Contractor's quality assurance plan and all reports prepared by the Contractor. The Employer's Representative is entitled to monitor, audit and spot check the Contractor's quality assurance procedure.

8.3   Inspection

8.3.1   The Contractor shall ensure that the Employer's Representative, and anyone authorised by the Employer's Representative, is able at all reasonable times to have access to all places where the Works are being executed [whether or not at the Site] and any place where any Works Items are produced, stored, extracted or prepared, or any other obligation of the Contractor under the Contract is being performed, and are able there to inspect, test, observe and examine all such items and activities.

8.3.2   The Contractor shall promptly give the Employer's Representative all particulars the Employer's Representative requests about the mode, place and time of manufacture, the source of supply and the performance capabilities of Works Items and any related information, including any test certificates that the Contract provides for.

8.3.3   The Contractor shall notify the Employer's Representative before any Works Item is covered or any Works Item that is to be inspected is packed or made impossible or difficult to inspect, in either case giving the Employer's Representative, and any person authorised by the Employer's Representative, a reasonable opportunity to inspect the Works Item.

> **NOTE**
>
> The Contractor is to give the Employer's Representative notice of when Work Items that require inspection are being covered up or packaged or made impossible or difficult to inspect. The Contractor shall notify the Employer's Representative and provide a reasonable opportunity for the inspection to take place.

8.4   Tests

8.4.1   The Contractor shall supply all Contractor's Things, documents, information, suitably qualified and experienced personnel, power, consumables and instruments required to carry out tests that the Contract requires the Contractor to do [both before and after Substantial Completion]. The Contractor shall agree with the Employer's Representative the time and place for these tests. The Employer's Representative, and others authorised by the Employer, may attend and observe the tests, and the Contractor shall facilitate their attendance and observation. Regardless of whether any Employer's Personnel attends, the Contractor shall promptly give the Employer's Representative a certified report of the result of every test.

8.4.2   If a test is failed, the Contractor may elect to repeat the test, or the Employer's Representative may require that the test be repeated. The Contractor shall, on request, pay the Employer any costs the Employer incurs as a result of any re-testing.

8.4.3   If the Contractor rectifies a Defect, it shall repeat any relevant test the Contract specifies for the relevant Works Item, if the Employer's Representative so directs.

> **NOTE**
>
> This sub-clause deals with the carrying out of all tests which the Contractor is required by the contract to do, both before and after substantial completion. The Contractor is to facilitate the attendance of the Employer's Representative to observe the tests, and to provide certified reports of result of each test. If a test fails the Contractor may elect to retest or be instructed by the Employer's Representative. The Contractor is responsible for the Employer's costs arising from any retest. If the Contractor repairs a defect for which he is at fault he shall repeat any relevant test to that Work if so requested by the Employer's Representative at the Contractor's cost.

8.5   Defects

8.5.1   The Employer's Representative may direct the Contractor to search for a Defect or suspected Defect or its cause. This may include uncovering, dismantling, re-covering and re-erecting work, providing facilities for tests, testing and inspecting. If, through searching or otherwise, the Contractor discovers a Defect, the Contractor shall notify the Employer's Representative as soon as practicable.

8.5.2   If, through notification or otherwise, the Employer's Representative becomes aware of a Defect, the Employer's Representative may direct the Contractor to do any of the following [or any combination of them]:

(1)   to remove the Works Item with the Defect from the Site

(2)   to demolish the Works Item with the Defect, if incorporated in the Works

(3)   to reconstruct, replace or correct the Works Item with the Defect

(4)   not to deliver the Works Item with the Defect to the Site.

8.5.3   The Contractor shall comply with any direction under this sub-clause 8.5 within the reasonable times, if any, the Employer's Representative directs. If the Contractor fails to begin the work required to comply with the direction within the reasonable time directed, if any, or to complete it as soon as practicable, the Employer may have the work done by others and the Contractor shall, on request, pay the Employer its cost of doing so.

8.5.4   Alternatively, the Contractor and the Employer's Representative may, with the Employer's consent, agree that the Employer will accept the Defect, either in whole or subject to any change to the Works Requirements that the Employer's Representative directs. In this case, the Contract Sum shall be reduced by the amount that, in the opinion of the Employer's Representative, is the resulting decrease in the value of the Works to the Employer. If the Employer's Representative notifies the Contractor that the Employer will not accept a Defect, this shall be conclusive.

8.5.5   The Employer's Representative may give a direction or rejection under this sub-clause 8.5 at any time before the Defects Certificate is issued. [The Contractor shall not be entitled to any adjustment to the Contract Sum or extension of time because of a direction given to deal with, or as a result of, a Defect or any other breach of the Contract by the Contractor.]

NOTE

This sub-clause deals with defects which now includes all workmanship and materials and Contractor's documentation which may not be in accordance with the Contract. In dealing with a defect there are five options open to the Employer's Representative:

(i)   Remove the work item with defect from the site

(ii)   Demolish work item with defect if incorporated in works

(iii) Reconstruct, replace or correct the works with the defect

(iv)   Not deliver the work items with the defect to the site

(v)   Alternatively, the Employer's Representative and the Contractor, with the Employer's agreement, may accept the defect either in whole or subject to any change in work requirements instructed by the Employer's Representative. Any resulting decrease in value of the Works shall be determined by the Employer's Representative and the amount shall be deducted from the contract sum. Such deduction may not relate solely to cost alone.

If the Employer's Representative will not accept a defect it shall be conclusive under this Contract.

No adjustment to cost or time are allowed for a defect which is the fault of the Contractor.

8.6   Defects Period

8.6.1   As soon as practicable after Substantial Completion of the Works or any Section, the Contractor shall complete any outstanding work and rectify any Defects that the Employer's Representative directs before the end of the Defects Period. In doing so, and in doing any tests after Substantial Completion, the Contractor shall cause as little disruption as possible to occupants and users of the Works.

8.6.2   If work remains outstanding or Defects remain uncorrected at the end of the Defects Period, or if the Contractor has completed outstanding work or rectified Defects after Substantial Completion of the Works or relevant Section and before the end of the Defects Period, the Employer's Representative may [without limiting the Employer's other rights] make an appropriate extension to the Defects Period. With the Employer's agreement the Employer's

Representative may, at the time that the Defects Period would have ended without this extension, issue an interim payment certificate conclusively making an appropriate reduction in retention, and the Contractor shall be entitled to invoice the Employer for that amount.

NOTE

Sub-clause 8.6 deals with the remedy of defects in the defects period. The Employer's Representative may, where serious defects have occurred during the defects period, seek to have the period extended to monitor the defects. The Contractor may agree and there will be an appropriate reduction to retention at the original defects completion date.

If no extension is agreed the Employer's Representative may, at the end of defects period, assess the risk that defects in the work item concerned may occur, or be noticed in the period from the remedial work to the works item and equal in length to the defects period, and make an appropriate deduction to the contract sum to compensate the Employer for that risk.

Sub-clause 8.6.2 (Defects Period) entitles the Employer's Representative to reduce the contract sum to compensate the Employer against the risk of defects occurring in the future.

8.7   Defects Certificate

The Employer's Representative shall issue the Defects Certificate to the Contractor and the Employer within 20 working days after the end of the Defects Period. [Nothing in this clause 8, nor any exercise or non-exercise by the Employer or the Employer's Representative of their rights under this clause 8, nor the Defects Certificate, relieves the Contractor of any obligation, except to the extent that a Defect is accepted by agreement under sub-clause 8.5.4.]

NOTE

The "Defects Certificate" means a certificate of the Employer's Representative issued to certify that the defects period has ended. The Employer's Representative shall issue this certificate to the Contractor and the Employer within 20 working days after the end of the defects period.

GENERAL NOTE ON SECTION

The works requirements will contain quality assurance procedures. The Contractor should establish and implement these requirements. The quality assurance procedures shall be reflected in the appropriate documents that the Contractor submits to the Employer's Representative. The Employer's Representative may monitor, carry out spot checks and audit the Contractor's quality assurance procedures.

The defects period means the period starting on substantial completion of the works and continuing for the period stated in the Schedule, Part 1, Section I (which, if none is stated, should taken to be one year) as may be extended under clause 8.6.2.

In the event that the Contractor does not agree with the amount of the reduction to the contract sum the Contractor can refer the issue to conciliation under sub-clause 13.1.

Where the defects period is extended there will also be issues with the release of the bond and maintaining insurances on the project. The Contractor will have to inform his bondsman and insurance agents.

9 TIME AND COMPLETION

9.1 Starting Date

9.1.1 The Contractor shall set the Starting Date, giving the Employer's Representative at least 15 working days notice, or any shorter period the Employer's Representative may agree, or any different period stated in the Works Requirements. The Starting Date shall, unless otherwise stated in the Works Requirements, be no more than 20 working days after the Contract Date.

9.1.2 Before the Starting Date [unless already given by the Contractor before the Contract Date, for example in response to a letter of intent] the Contractor shall give the Employer all of the following, all executed, as relevant, by the relevant persons:

(1) the Agreement

(2) a performance bond, if required by the Contract

(3) if the Works Requirements state that the Contractor or the Contractor's nominee is to be appointed as project supervisor for the construction stage, the required appointment, and the developed safety and health plan required by the Construction Regulations

(4) evidence that the insurances required by the Contract are in effect

(5) any collateral warranties required by the Contract

However, collateral warranties may be given on a later date that the Employer's Representative has agreed to.

9.1.3 On the Starting Date, the Contractor shall start to execute the Works on the Site. The Contractor shall, unless the Employer's Representative directs otherwise, proceed regularly and diligently in order to achieve Substantial Completion of the Works and each Section by its Date for Substantial Completion.

NOTE

Sub-clause 9.1 deals with the starting date. Notice of 15 working day must be given to the Employer's Representative, or any shorter period agreed, or as per the work requirements.

Unless it is otherwise stated in the work requirements, the starting date shall be no later than 20 working days after the contract date.

The Contractor must comply with the following obligations before the starting date:

(i) Executing the agreement;

(ii) Providing the performance bond, if required;

(iii) If required under the work requirements, confirming acceptance of the appointment as project supervisor for the construction stage, and providing a copy of the developed health and safety plan;

(iv) Providing evidence that the insurances required by the contract is in place;

(v) Providing collateral warranties required, though they may be deferred to later date by the Employer's Representative, or as per the Schedule;

(vi) Ensuring that his organisation is prepared and ready to have these documents in place.

It may be necessary to work under a "letter of intent" as contained in the Model Forms. The Contractor should ensure that any letter of intent provides for the Contractor to be paid for all works and documents produced in the event that the project is delayed or cancelled.

9.2   Suspension

9.2.1 The Employer's Representative may at any time direct the Contractor to suspend all or part of the work under the Contract. The Contractor shall comply with the direction and, during suspension, shall protect, store and secure the affected Works Items against deterioration, loss and damage and maintain the Insurances.

9.2.2 After a suspension under clause 9.2.1, the Contractor shall resume work when so directed by the Employer's Representative. When a direction to resume is given, the Contractor and the Employer's Representative shall jointly examine the Works and Works Items affected by the suspension. If the Contractor is entitled to an adjustment of the Contract Sum or an extension of time because of the suspension, the Contractor's cost of rectifying any deterioration in or loss of the Works or Work Items that the Contractor could not have avoided shall be included in the determination of the adjustment, and any resulting delay shall be taken into account in determining the extension.

9.2.3 If a suspension, that did not result from a breach of the Contractor's obligations, has continued for more than 3 months, the Contractor may request the Employer's Representative's permission to proceed. If the Employer's Representative does not give permission within 28 days after being requested to do so, the Contractor may, by giving notice to the Employer's Representative

(1) if the suspension affects part of the Works, treat the suspension as a Change Order to omit that part of the Works or

(2) if the suspension affects the whole of the Works, give notice to terminate the Contractor's obligation to complete the Works under the Contract.

NOTE

The Employer may suspend the works. In the event of a suspension the works have to be protected, stored and kept secure. The works will be resumed on instruction from the Employer's Representative. The Contractor is entitled to the cost of any remedial works. The Contractor is entitled to an adjustment of the contract sum and an extension of time, both of which have to be assessed.

Suspension under 9.2 is a delay and compensation event (Item 3 of the Schedule, Part 1, Section K). Costs are calculated at the daily delay rate quoted by the Contractor in the Schedule (Part 2, Section D). These costs may not cover the Contractor's full costs, e.g. costs from subcontractors and offsite storage and the like.

If the suspension lasts more than three months then the Contractor may treat the instruction to suspend as an instruction to omit that part of the Works or give notice to terminate the Contractor's obligations under the Contract.

9.3   Delay and Extension of Time

9.3.1 If the Contractor becomes aware that work under the Contract is being or is likely to be delayed for any reason, it shall as soon as practicable notify the Employer's Representative of the delay and its cause. As soon as practicable after that, and in any event within 40 working days after the Contractor became aware of the delay, the Contractor shall give the Employer's Representative full details of the delay and its effect on the progress of the Works. But if the Contractor has given notice and details of the delay under sub-clause 10.3.1 it does not have to give notice or details again under this sub-clause 9.3.1 for the same delay. In any event, the Contractor shall promptly give any further information about the delay the Employer's Representative directs.

NOTE

Sub-clause 9.3 is a critical clause. In order to retain any rights to receive extensions and costs to cover resulting delay, the Contractor's organisation needs to follow it to the letter.

Under sub-clause 9.3.1, where the Contractor is aware that the work is being or is likely to be delayed for any reason, he shall, as soon as is practicable, notify the Employer's Representative of the delay and cause.

At 40 working days, at the most, after the event he shall give to the Employer's Representative full details of delay and its effect on progress and promptly supply any further information on the delay requested by the Employer's Representative.

Note that this means any delay, not just those to which an entitlement to an extension of time is given.

9.3.2   If Substantial Completion of the Works or any Section has been, is being or will be delayed beyond the Date for Substantial Completion by a Delay Event and if all of the following apply:

(1)   the Delay Event is not a result of the Contractor's or Contractor's Personnel's act or omission or the Contractor's breach of the Contract

(2)   the Contractor cannot avoid the delay and makes all reasonable efforts to minimise the delay

(3)   the Contract does not provide otherwise

then, subject to this sub-clause 9.3, sub-clause 9.4 and clause 10, there shall be an extension to the Date for Substantial Completion of the Works and any affected Section equal to the amount of the delay beyond the Date for Substantial Completion caused by the Delay Event taking into account only Site Working Days. The Contractor and the Employer's Representative shall follow the procedure in clause 10.

NOTE

Sub-clause 9.3.2 deals with delay to the substantial completion date of whole or part of the works which has been, is being or will be affected. The delays must not be the result of an act, omission or breach of contract by the Contractor. The delay event must be one that could not be avoided. The Contractor has to make all reasonable efforts to mitigate the delay.

The clause states that subject to sub clause 9.3 and 9.4 there shall be an extension to the substantial completion date of the whole or the section equal to the amount of delay taking into account site working days only.

The Employer's Representative may act on own initiative in that he does not need to wait for notice if he considers an extension is due. This is, we presume, to protect the Employer's right to an extension of time.

All claims for extensions of time must be processed under clause 10.3. Failure to do so will defeat any entitlement.

9.3.3   The Employer's Representative may, at any time, revise a determination of an extension to the Date for Substantial Completion of the Works or any Section, but shall not bring those dates forward except by agreement with the Contractor under sub-clause 9.5 when work has been omitted.

NOTE

Under sub-clause 9.3.3 the Employer's Representative may review an assessment at any time but may not bring the substantial completion date forward except with the Contractor's agreement under sub-clause 9.5 where works are omitted.

9.4   Programme Contingency

9.4.1   The Contractor has included in the initial Contract Sum and shall include in its programme a contingency for delays to the Date for Substantial Completion of the Works caused by Compensation Events.

9.4.2   If the total number of Site Working Days' delay to Substantial Completion of the Works caused by Compensation Events (for which the Contractor would otherwise be entitled to an extension) is less than the programme contingency threshold in the Schedule, part 1K, there shall be no extensions to the initial Date for Substantial Completion of the Works for delay caused by Compensation Events.

9.4.3   If the total number of Site Working Days' delay to Substantial Completion of the Works caused by Compensation Events (for which the Contractor would otherwise be entitled to an extension) exceeds the programme contingency threshold in the Schedule, part 1K, the number of Site Working Days stated as that threshold shall be deducted from the total number of Site Working Days' extension to the initial Date for Substantial Completion of the Works for delay caused by Compensation Events.

9.4.4   [This sub-clause 9.4 does not apply to extensions to the Date for Substantial Completion of a Section, nor to extensions of time resulting from Delay Events that are not Compensation Events.]

9.4.5   Use of the programme contingency provided for in this sub-clause shall be claimed and determined in accordance with this clause 9 and clause 10. In making a determination under sub-clauses 9.3 and 10.5 in respect of a delay to Substantial Completion of the Works, the Employer's Representative shall notify the Contractor and the Employer of how much of the programme contingency threshold has been used-up by delays to Substantial Completion of the Works caused by Compensation Events.

NOTE

This condition provides the Employer the opportunity to "buy out" a numbers of days delay. This is referred to as the "programme contingency". The contingency for delays has to be built into the programme time and the associated costs have to be included in the tender sum. The amount of contingency days will be given to the Contractor in the Schedule, Part 1K, at tender stage. Before an extension of time is granted the days in the threshold contingency must be exceeded.

The delays must arise from compensation events only. The compensation events will be detailed by the Employer in the Schedule, Part 1, Section K.

The Contractor records and provides to the Employer's Representative details of the delays and their effect. The Employer's Representative makes the final assessment under clause 10.5.

The Employer's Representative shall notify the Contractor and the Employer of how much of the threshold is used up by the delays to the date for substantial completion caused by compensation events.

9.5   Omissions and Reduction of Time

If a Change Order omits any of the Works, and the omission will result, or has resulted, in a reduction of the time required to complete the Works or any Section, the Date for Substantial Completion shall be reduced by any amount agreed between the Employer's Representative and the Contractor. [If there is no agreement, there shall be no reduction.]

> **NOTE**
>
> The date for substantial completion can be brought forward as a result of a change order arising from an omission. The reduction in the contract time to complete the works has to be agreed with the Contractor: without agreement the date for substantial completion cannot be brought forward.

9.6   Substantial Completion

9.6.1   The Contractor shall achieve Substantial Completion of the Works and each Section by its Date for Substantial Completion.

9.6.2   Within 20 working days after receiving the Contractor's request to certify Substantial Completion of the Works or a Section, the Employer's Representative shall give to the Contractor and the Employer

(1)   a certificate stating the date that Substantial Completion occurred or

(2)   the reasons for not issuing the certificate.

But if the Schedule, part 1H, so states, the Employer's Representative shall not be required to certify Substantial Completion of the Works or a Section before its Date for Substantial Completion. The certificate may include a list of Defects and any outstanding work [but nothing in the certificate, including the failure to list any Defect, relieves the Contractor of any obligations].

> **NOTE**
>
> The Contractor must request the Employer's Representative to issue a "Certificate of Substantial Completion for the Works" or a "Section of the Works". The Employer's Representative has 20 working days after receiving the request to issue the certificate stating the date that substantial completion was achieved or to state the reasons for not issuing the certificate. Part 1H of the Schedule can state that the Employer's Representative does not have to issue the certificate for a date earlier than the substantial completion date stated in the contract.
>
> The certificate may include a list of defects or incomplete works that the Contractor has to make good or complete.

9.7   (sub-clause not used)

9.8   Liquidated Damages

9.8.1   If the Works do not reach Substantial Completion by the Date for Substantial Completion of the Works, the Contractor shall pay the Employer [and the Employer may deduct from payments to the Contractor] liquidated damages calculated at the rate stated in the Schedule, part 1G, for the period from the Date for Substantial Completion of the Works to the date of substantial completion of the Works.

9.8.2   If a Section does not reach Substantial Completion by its Date for Substantial Completion, the Contractor shall pay to the Employer liquidated damages calculated at the rate stated in the Schedule for the period from the Date for Substantial Completion of the Section to the date of substantial completion of the Section (or, if earlier and if the Schedule states a rate of liquidated damages for the Works, to the Date for Substantial Completion of the Works).

9.8.3   In this sub-clause 9.8 **date of substantial completion** means the date certified by the Employer's Representative that the Works or Section reached Substantial Completion.

NOTE

If the works do not reach substantial completion by the stated date the Contractor shall pay the Employer, or the Employer may deduct from payments due to the Contractor, liquidated damages calculated at the rate stated in Part 1G of the Schedule. Liquidated damages may also apply to a section or sections of the works.

In the event that the Employer's Representative does not issue the certificate of substantial completion as a result of incomplete works, as advised in accordance with clause 9.6.2(2), then the Contractor is exposed to liquidated damages from the Employer.

GENERAL NOTES ON SECTION

Delay and Extension of Time – The Contractor shall, as soon as he becomes aware that the works are being or are likely to be delayed, must notify the Employer's Representative of the delay and the cause. Within 40 days after becoming aware of the delay the Contractor shall provide full details of the delay and the effect on progress of the works to the Employer's Representative.

While Condition 9.3.1 requires the Contractor to give notice of delay to the Employer's Representative, the claim for the extension of time and/or costs must be given under Condition 10.3.1, and any notice under 10.3.1 must prominently state that it is being given under Condition 10.3.

The time restraints, i.e. 40 working days after the Contractor became aware of the delay (not the notice), must be strictly adhered to.

The Employer's Representative extends the date for substantial completion under sub-clause 9.3.2.

In the event that a Contractor has already provided a notice and details of a delay for an event under Condition 10.3.1 the Contractor does not have to give a notice under Condition 9.3.1 for the same delay.

10 CLAIMS AND ADJUSTMENTS

10.1 Compensation Event

10.1.1 Subject to and in accordance with this sub-clause 10.1, if a Compensation Event occurs the Contract Sum shall be adjusted by the amount provided in sub-clause 10.6. However, the Contract Sum shall be increased only to the extent that all of the following apply to the Compensation Event:

(1) The Compensation Event is not a result of the Contractor's or Contractor's Personnel's act or omission or the Contractor's breach of the Contract

(2) The Contractor cannot avoid the adverse effects of the Compensation Event and makes all reasonable efforts to minimise them

(3) The Contractor has complied with this clause 10 in full [including giving notices and details within the time required]

(4) The Contract does not provide otherwise.

10.1.2 The Contractor's sole remedies for a Compensation Event shall be those stated in the Contract.

10.2 Contractor to Pay Employer's Cost of Checking Quantities

The Contractor shall pay the Employer's cost of having a check done if the Contractor calls for an adjustment to the Contract Sum because of a difference between the Contract value of the Works according to the quantities and descriptions in a Bill of Quantities (if any) in the Pricing Document and the Contract value of the Works according to the Works Requirements (when this is a Compensation Event), and it is found that no increase is to be made to the Contract Sum.

10.3 Contractor Claims

10.3.1 If the Contractor considers that under the Contract there should be an extension of time or an adjustment to the Contract Sum, or that it has any other entitlement under or in connection with the Contract, the Contractor shall, as soon as practicable and in any event within 20 working days after it became aware, or should have become aware, of something that could result in such an entitlement, give notice of this to the Employer's Representative. The notice must be given according to sub-clause 4.14 and prominently state that it is being given under sub-clause 10.3 of the Contract. Within a further 20 working days after giving the notice, the Contractor shall give the Employer's Representative details of all of the following:

(1) all relevant facts about the claim

(2) a detailed calculation and, so far as practicable, a proposal, based on that calculation, of any adjustment to be made to the Contract Sum and of the amount of any other entitlement claimed by the Contractor

(3) if the Contractor considers that the programme contingency referred to in sub-clause 9.4 should be used or that there should be an extension of time, the information required under sub-clause 9.3, and, so far as practicable, a proposal, based on that information for any use of the programme contingency or any extension to the Date for Substantial Completion of the Works and any affected Section. The Contractor shall give any further information about the event or circumstance requested by the Employer's Representative.

10.3.2   If the Contractor does not give notice and details in accordance with and within the time provided in this sub-clause 10.3, except where the Contractor has been required to and has given a proposal complying in full with sub-clause 10.4 [notwithstanding anything else in the Contract] the Contractor shall not be entitled to an increase to the Contract Sum or extension of time or use of the programme contingency referred to in sub-clause 9.4 [and the Employer shall be released from all liability to the Contractor in connection with the matter].

10.3.3   If the cause of the claim has a continuing effect, the Contractor shall update the information at monthly intervals

(1)   stating the extension of time and adjustment to the Contract Sum claimed for delay and cost already incurred and

(2)   so far as practicable, proposing a final adjustment to the Contract Sum and Date for Substantial Completion of the Works and any affected Section and

(3)   providing any other information the Employer's Representative reasonably requires.

10.3.4   The Contractor shall keep detailed contemporary records to substantiate any aspect of an event or circumstance about which it has given, or is entitled to give, notice under this subclause 10.3, and its resulting costs. These shall include any records the Employer's Representative directs the Contractor to keep. The Contractor shall give the records to the Employer's Representative if so directed.

NOTE

There are 15 compensation events listed in the Schedule, Part 1, Section K. Item 17 is normally a compensation event. Should a compensation event arise, then before the contract sum is adjusted by the Employer's Representative the following criteria must be satisfied:

(i)   The compensation event is not a result of an act or omission of the Contractor or Contractor's Personnel, or the Contractor's breach of the contract;

(ii)   The Contractor cannot avoid the adverse effects of the compensation event and makes all reasonable efforts to minimise them;

(iii)   The Contractor has complied with this clause 10 in full (including giving notices and details within the time required);

(iv)   The Contract does not provide otherwise.

If the Contractor considers that there should be an extension of time or an adjustment to the contract sum, or if any other entitlement exists, he shall provide such notice to the Employer's Representative within 20 working days after he becomes aware, or should have been aware of something that would give rise to an entitlement. The notice must comply with Condition 4.14 (Communications) and be sent to the person identified in the Schedule, Part 1, Section A. The notice must prominently state that it is being given under sub-clause 10.3.

Within a further 20 working days the Contractor shall provide:

(i)   All relevant facts;

(ii)   A detailed calculation and a proposal based on the calculation of the adjustment to be made to the contract sum and of the amount of any other entitlement claimed by the Contractor;

(iii)   Details of the amount of the contingency referred to in sub-clause 9.4 to be used, or details of the effect on programme and completion dates.

The Employer's Representative may request the Contractor to provide further information.

If the Contractor does not comply with notices, details and time scales set down in sub-clause 10.3 then the Contractor shall not be entitled to an increase in the contract sum or an extension of time and the Employer shall be released from all liability to the Contractor in relation to the matter.

Contractors must comply with all the requirements of the Contract as set down in Conditions 9 and 10 if they are to avail of entitlements in relation to extensions of time, compensation events and adjustments to the Contract. This places obligations on Contractors to maintain records and notices to a far greater degree than existed under the current GDLA and IEI Contracts. The Contractor's obligation is also set out in Condition 10.3.4.

If the cause of the claim has a continuing effect the Contractor shall update all the information at monthly intervals. The Contractor will have to:

  (i)   state the extension of time and adjustment to the contract sum claimed in respect of any delay and cost already incurred;

  (ii)   Propose a final adjustment to the contract sum and the date for substantial completion of the works and any affected section;

  (iii) Provide any other information that the Employer's Representative requires.

Sub-clause 10.3.4 requires the Contractor to keep contemporary records of all events under clause 10.3. The Employer's Representative may instruct the Contractor to keep such records.

10.4   Proposed Instructions

The Employer's Representative may direct the Contractor to make proposals for a proposed instruction. The Contractor shall not implement the proposed instruction unless and until the Employer's Representative has confirmed the instruction as given. Within 20 working days after the Employer's Representative directs the Contractor to make proposals, the Contractor shall give to the Employer's Representative all of the following:

(1) a detailed calculation and proposal, based on the calculation, of any adjustment to the Contract Sum that would result from the proposed instruction

(2) if the proposed instruction would cause a delay, the information required under sub-clause 9.3, and a proposal, based on that information for any use of the programme contingency referred to in sub-clause 9.4 or extension to the Date for Substantial Completion of the Works and any affected Section

(3) if the proposed instruction is to omit any of the Works, a revised programme and, if appropriate, a proposed earlier Date for Substantial Completion of the Works and any affected Section

(4) any Contractor's Documents required in connection with the proposed instruction, or a timetable for them.

NOTE

The Employer's Representative may request the Contractor to provide a proposal on a proposed instruction. The Contractor has 20 working days to provide the details, which will include:

  (i)   Calculation of the adjustment to the contract sum;

  (ii)   Details of any delay and information required under clause 9.3 with regards to the date for substantial completion of the works or any section of the works;

  (iii) A revised programme in the case of an omission, and, if appropriate, a proposed earlier date for substantial completion;

  (iv)   Contractor's documents required in relation to the proposal or a timetable for them.

The Contractor shall not implement the proposed instruction until the Employer's Representative confirms the instruction as given.

10.5   Employer's Representative's Determination

10.5.1   If the Contractor has made a claim or proposal under sub-clauses 10.3 or 10.4, the Employer's Representative shall, within 20 working days of receiving it, do one of the following:

(1)   direct the Contractor to give additional information or revised proposals, in which case the Contractor shall do so within 10 working days and the Employer's Representative shall reply in accordance with this sub-clause within a further 10 working days, but that reply must not require the Contractor to give additional information or a revised proposal

(2)   notify the Contractor and the Employer that the Contractor's proposals are agreed and make any resulting adjustments to the Contract Sum, use of the programme contingency referred to in sub-clause 9.4 or extension to the Date for Substantial Completion of the Works and any affected Section

(3)   make a determination of any adjustments to the Contract Sum, use of the programme contingency referred to in sub-clause 9.4 or extension to the Date for Substantial Completion of the Works and any affected Section, and notify the Contractor and the Employer

(4)   in response to a proposal under sub-clause 10.4, notify the Contractor that the proposed instruction will not be given.

10.5.2   The Employer's Representative may [but is not bound to] determine an extension of time for a Compensation Event that is a breach of the Contract by the Employer on its own initiative even if the Contractor has not made a claim or proposal under sub-clauses 10.3 or 10.4.

NOTE

The Employer's Representative has 20 working days to respond to a Contractor's claim under sub-clause 10.3 or a proposal under sub-clause 10.4. He may:

(i)   Request more information or a revised proposal – the Contractor then has 10 working to respond. The Employer's Representative then has a further 10 working days to reply;

(ii)   Notify the Employer and the Contractor that the Contractor's proposals are agreed and make any resulting adjustment to the Contract Sum, use of the programme contingency referred to in sub-clause 9.4, or extension to the date of substantial completion of the works and any affected section;

(iii)   Make a determination of the adjustment to the contract sum, use of the programme contingency referred to in sub-clause 9.4, or extension to the date of substantial completion of the works and any affected section and notify the Contractor and the Employer;

(iv)   In response to a Contractor's proposal issued under sub-clause 10.4, notify the Contractor that the proposed instruction will not be given.

Where the Contractor has not made a claim under sub-clause 10.3 or submitted a proposal under sub-clause 10.4, the Employer's Representative may work (but is not bound to) on his own initiative in making an adjustment to the contract sum or extending the date for substantial completion of the works.

10.6   Adjustments to the Contract Sum

Adjustments to the Contract Sum for a Compensation Event shall only be for the value of any additional, substituted, and omitted work required as a result of the Compensation Event under this sub-clause 10.6 and any delay cost under sub-clause 10.7. Additional, substituted, and omitted work shall be valued as follows:

10.6.1   If the Compensation Event requires additional, substituted or omitted work, similar to work for which there are rates in the Pricing Document, to be executed under similar conditions, the determination shall use those rates.

10.6.2   If the Compensation Event requires additional, substituted or omitted work that is not similar to work for which there are rates in the Pricing Document, or is not to be executed under similar conditions, the determination shall be on the basis of the rates in the Pricing Document when that is reasonable.

10.6.3   If the adjustment cannot be determined under the above rules, the Employer's Representative shall make a fair valuation.

10.6.4   The Employer's Representative may conclusively direct that additional or substituted work required as a result of a Compensation Event be determined (in full or in part) on the basis of the cost of performing the additional or substituted work, compared with the Contractor's cost without the Compensation Event, determined as follows:

(1)   the number of hours worked or to be worked by each category of work person stated in the Schedule, part 2D, and engaged on the work to which the Compensation Event relates, on or off the Site, multiplied in each case by the tendered hourly rate for that category stated in the Schedule, part 2D and

(2)   the cost of materials used in that work, taking into account discounts and excluding VAT, plus the percentage adjustment tendered by the Contractor and stated in the Schedule, part 2D and

(3)   the cost of plant reasonably used for that work, whether hired or owned by the Contractor, at the rates in the document listed in the Schedule, part 1K (as that document may be modified according to the Schedule, part 1K) plus or minus the percentage adjustment tendered by the Contractor and included in the Schedule, part 2D. If the document listed in the Schedule does not give a rate for a plant item, a market rental rate shall be used, plus or minus the percentage adjustment.

NOTE

The adjustment to the contract sum for a compensation event is carried out by using rates contained in the pricing document, fair rates or recorded hours by the rates stated in the Schedule, Part 2 D, together with the cost of plant and materials with the percentage additions quoted in the Schedule, Part 2 D.

The Employer's Representative may direct that additional or substituted works required as a result of a compensation event be determined in accordance with the Contractor's tendered hourly labour rates and the Contractor's tendered percentage addition to the cost of plant and materials.

10.7   Delay Cost

10.7.1   If the Date for Substantial Completion of the Works has been extended because of a Compensation Event [and not otherwise, and subject to sub-clause 10.7.2], there shall be added to the Contract Sum an amount for delay cost, either (whichever it says in the Schedule, part 1K)

(1)   for each Site Working Day for which the Date for Substantial Completion of the Works has been extended because of the Compensation Event, the daily rate of delay cost tendered by the Contractor in the Schedule, part 2D or

(2)   the expenses [excluding profit and loss of profit] unavoidably incurred by the Contractor as a result of the delay to the Date for Substantial Completion of the Works caused by the Compensation Event in respect of which that date has been extended under the Contract.

10.7.2   If a delay has more than one cause, and one or more of the causes is not a Compensation Event, there shall be no increase to the Contract Sum for delay cost for the period of concurrent delay.

> **NOTE**
>
> Sub-clause 10.7.2 provides that if a delay has more than one cause, and one or more of the causes is not a compensation event, there shall be no increase to the contract sum for delay costs for the period of concurrent delay. This removes any dispute or ambiguity about which delay is the dominant delay and whether compensation is due to the Contractor as a result of the dominant delay.

10.7.3   Except as provided in this sub-clause 10.7 [notwithstanding anything else in the Contract] losses or expenses arising from or in connection with delay, disruption, loss of productivity or knock-on effect shall not be taken into account or included in any increase to the Contract Sum, and the Employer shall have no liability for such losses or expenses.

10.7.4   [There shall be no delay cost paid as a result of extensions to the Date for Substantial Completion of a Section].

10.7.5   If the Schedule states more than one rate for delay cost, the rate for the period when the delay occurred or delayed part of the Works shall be used. This shall be determined by the Employer's Representative.

> **NOTE**
>
> Delay costs are added as defined in the Schedule, Part 2 D. The Contractor's delay costs are capped to that stated in the Schedule.
>
> Losses or expenses arising from or in relation to delay, disruption, loss of productivity or knock-on effect shall not be taken into account or included in any assessment of an increase to the contract sum. The Employer has no liability for such losses or expenses.
>
> There will be no delay costs paid as a result of extensions to the date for substantial completion of a section.

10.8   Price Variation

The Contract includes clause PV1 attached.

> **NOTE**
>
> Sub-clause 10.8 deals with price variation. The "Proven Cost Method" (PV1);
>
> This is an invoice-based system whereby the Contractor establishes his entitlement after the fixed-price period by invoices which are checked by the Employer. The definition of "Base Date" under PV1 is the first day of the thirty-first month after the Contract date, so that this approach guarantees the Employer the 30-month fixed price even if there should be a delay in setting the contract date.

10.9   Employer's Claims

10.9.1   If the Employer or the Employer's Representative considers that, under the Contract, there should be a reduction of the Contract Sum, or that any amount is due to the Employer from the Contractor under the Contract, the Employer or the Employer's Representative shall, as soon as practicable, give notice and particulars of the event or circumstances to the other, and to the Contractor. The notice shall include

(1)   details of the event or circumstances giving rise to the notice, and all relevant facts and

(2)   a calculation, and a proposal based on that calculation, of any adjustment to be made to the Contract Sum or any amount due by the Contractor to the Employer.

10.9.2 The Contractor shall be entitled, within 20 working days of receipt of such a notice, to give a response to the Employer's Representative and shall, if the notice was given by the Employer, give a copy of any response to the Employer. Within 20 working days after receiving the Contractor's response, or after the time for responding has elapsed, if the Contractor has not responded within that time, the Employer's Representative shall determine the matter in accordance with the Contract.

10.9.3 The Employer may deduct from any amount due to the Contractor

(1) any amount determined by the Employer's Representative to be due, or likely to become due, from the Contractor to the Employer under the Contract and

(2) any amount due from the Contractor to the Employer under any contract.

10.9.4 The procedure in this sub-clause 10.9 shall apply until either the Defects Certificate or the certificates required following termination have been issued, but this does not limit the Employer's rights after then.

NOTE

The Contractor can be liable to the Employer for any monies the Employer or the Employer's Representative may consider due to the Employer. The Contractor shall pay these monies to the Employer or the Employer may deduct the money from payments on the particular project or any other contract.

The Employer's claims are not time-barred as the Contractor's are under sub-clause 10.3. The Contractor has 20 working days to respond to such a notice to the Employer's Representative and the Employer (if the notice was sent by the Employer). The Employer Representative has 20 working days to consider the matter.

Notice of the event and a calculation of the adjustment to the contract sum must be provided to the Contractor by either the Employer or the Employer's Representative before any adjustments can be made to the contract sum.

GENERAL NOTES ON SECTION

This clause deals with the manner in which both delay events and compensation costs will be evaluated. This is an innovative approach to the management of claims, requiring strict adherence to procedures in order to preserve an entitlement to claim.

Every single event in respect of which compensation is to be claimed must be processed under sub-clause 10.3. The amount of detail required is substantial and where the claim arises, for example, from an instructed variation, the requirement and responsibility to furnish the notice and the documentation rests with the Contractor. Notices, within the specified time periods, must be submitted in order to preserve entitlements.

Schedule 1, Section K, is central to the contract, as the lists contained in the Schedule set out when compensation will be payable and when extensions of time can be granted. If the event does not appear on the list in the Schedule no compensation will be payable nor will extensions to the date for substantial completion be made.

Sub-clause 10.4 provides that, prior to issuing an instruction, the Employer's Representative can instruct the Contractor to prepare an assessment, in terms of time and money, of a proposed instruction. The Contractor should note the additional burden placed upon him in the preparation of documents and programmes for a work item that may not proceed. There is no provision for the Employer to compensate the Contractor for any administration work or associated costs.

In practical terms this is a "Fixed Price Lump Sum Contract" which does not allow for price variation in any meaningful way except for increases in PRSI, VAT and excise duties which can be reimbursed at costs.

11   PAYMENT

11.1   Interim Payment

11.1.1   At each of the following times

(i)   the periods for interim payment stated in the Schedule, part 1L, if the amount payable is more than the minimum amount stated in the Schedule and

(ii)   upon issue of the certificate of Substantial Completion for the Works or any Section the Contractor shall give a statement to the Employer's Representative showing all of the following:

(1)   the progress of the Works

(2)   the instalment of the Contract Sum that the Contractor considers should, under the Contract, be paid on an interim basis

(3)   a detailed breakdown

(4)   any supporting evidence the Employer's Representative requires.

The statement given on Substantial Completion shall include all amounts due to the Contractor for the Works or Section.

11.1.2   The instalment of the Contract Sum that the Contractor shall be entitled to be paid on an interim basis shall be

(1)   the Contract value of the Works properly executed by the Contractor [according to the Pricing Document, as a portion of the Contract Sum] and

(2)   any amount the Employer's Representative considers proper under sub-clause 11.2 and

(3)   amounts for adjustments to the Contract Sum for Compensation Events, as determined under the Contract and

(4)   any amount to be paid according to clause PV1 attached.

11.1.3   Within 10 working days of receipt of the Contractor's statement the Employer's Representative shall give the Contractor a certificate, sending a copy to the Employer, setting out the amount of interim payment that, in the Employer's Representative's opinion, is to be made by the Employer to the Contractor, taking account of retention under subclause 11.3 and deductions and amounts due from the Contractor to the Employer [including damages for delay and charges referred to in sub-clause 7.12 and deductions under subclause 11.4], together with calculations and the reasons for the opinion.

11.1.4   If there is a sum due to the Contractor, the Contractor shall send an invoice to the Employer for that sum after receiving the interim certificate. The Employer shall pay the amount due on the invoice within 15 working days after receiving the invoice.

NOTE

The time of interim payments will be stated in Part 1 L of the Schedule. At the time for an interim payment the Contractor shall provide to the Employer's Representative a statement showing:

(i)   the progress of the Works;

(ii)   the instalment that the Contractor should be paid;

(iii)   a detailed breakdown;

(iv)   any supporting details the Employer's Representative requires.

Not stated in sub-clause 11.1.2 but contained in sub-clause 5.3.7, the Contractor must supply with each interim statement a certificate stating that the Contractor has complied in full with sub-clause 5.3 (Pay and Conditions of Employment); see sub-clause 11.4.4 for the severe effect of non-compliance with sub-clause 5.3.7.

Within 10 days of receipt of the Contractor's interim statement the Employer's Representative shall issue a Certificate setting out the amounts due to the Contractor (if any) after taking account of any amount due from the Contractor to the Employer and charges referred to in sub-clause 7.12. The Employer's Representative has to provide the calculations and reasons for his opinion in support of the certificate.

The Contractor has to provide an invoice to the Employer for any amount due to him as directed by the payment certificate. The Employer then pays the amount within 15 days after receipt of the invoice.

11.2   Unfixed Works Items

At the discretion of the Employer's Representative, but only when so provided in the Schedule, part 1L, interim payments may include any amount, not exceeding the percentage of value stated in the Schedule, part 1L, the Employer's Representative considers proper for each of the following:

(1)   the Contract value of any Works Items that comply with all of the following requirements, all to the satisfaction of the Employer's Representative:

    (a)   they have been completed and are substantially ready to be incorporated in the Works

    (b)   title to them has been vested in the Employer

    (c)   they are stored suitably at the Site

    (d)   they have not been delivered to the Site prematurely

(2)   the Contract value of any Work Items not delivered to the Site that comply with all of the following requirements, all to the satisfaction of the Employer's Representative:

    (a)   they have been completed and are substantially ready to be incorporated in the Works

    (b)   title to them has been vested in the Employer

    (c)   they are stored suitably and set aside and marked to show clearly that their destination is the Site and that they are the property of the Employer

    (d)   they are clearly identified in a list given to the Employer's Representative, together with documentary evidence that title is vested in the Employer

    (e)   they are insured as required by the Contract, and will be insured as required while in transit

    (f)   the Contractor has given the Employer a bond in the form for such bonds in the Works Requirements, or if there is none, a form approved by the Employer, executed by a surety approved by the Employer's Representative, for the amount to be paid.

In this clause 11.2, the Contract value of a Works Item means a portion of the Contract Sum the Employer's Representative determines is for supplying of the Works Item, having regard to the Pricing Document. [If the Pricing Document has a rate or price for supplying and fixing a Works Item, the Contract value includes only the portion for supplying the Works Item, as determined by the Employer's Representative.]

NOTE

The Contractor can be paid for unfixed works Items up to a value of 90 percent provided that the Contract allows a provision for a higher value which will be detailed in Part 1L of the Schedule, provided that:

(i)   they have been completed and they are substantially ready to be incorporated into the Works;

(ii)   title to them has been vested in the Employer;

(iii)   they are stored suitably on site;

(iv)   they have not been brought to the site prematurely.

Payment for unfixed work items is at the discretion of the Employer's Representative.

Payment for goods not delivered to the site is governed by the following:

(i)   they have been completed and are substantially ready to be incorporated in the works;

(ii)   title to them has been vested in the Employer;

(iii)   they are stored suitably and marked to show that they are the property of the Employer and that their destination is the site;

(iv)   they are clearly identified in a list provided to the Employer's Representative and with documentary evidence that title is vested in the Employer;

(v)   they are insured as required by the Contract and will be insured while in transit;

(vi)   the Employer is provided with a bond by a surety approved by the Employer's Representative for the amount to be paid.

11.3   Retention

11.3.1   There shall be deducted from each interim payment to the Contractor the retention percentage stated in the Schedule, part 1L.

11.3.2   Upon issue of the certificate of Substantial Completion of the Works, the Contractor shall be entitled to invoice the Employer for half of the amount so retained. Upon the issue of the Defects Certificate, the Contractor shall be entitled to invoice the Employer for the balance of the money so retained.

11.3.3   If, within 10 working days of the issue of the certificate of Substantial Completion of the Works, or another date agreed by the Employer's Representative, the Contractor provides to the Employer a retention bond in the form in the Work Requirements, or, if there is none, a form approved by the Employer, for the amount retained by the Employer, and executed by a surety approved by the Employer, the Contractor shall be entitled to invoice the Employer for the balance of the money retained.

11.3.4   Upon issue of the certificate of Substantial Completion of a Section of the Works, the retention amount to be withheld until issue of the certificate of Substantial Completion of the Works shall be reduced by the amount stated in the Schedule, part 1G, and the Contractor shall be entitled to invoice the Employer for that amount.

11.3.5   The Employer shall pay the Contractor the amount due on an invoice under this sub-clause 11.3 within 15 working days after receiving the invoice [less any amount that the Employer is entitled to deduct according to sub-clause 10.9].

11.4   Full Payment

The payments to the Contractor under this Contract are for compliance in full with the Contractor's obligations to the time of payment [including construction management, programming, reporting, payment of wages and observing employment requirements] [but payment does not imply acceptance that the obligations have been performed]. When the Contractor has not fully complied with its obligations, the Employer is not required to make payment in full [without limiting its other rights or remedies]. In particular

11.4.1 If the Contractor has not given a collateral warranty by the date stated in the Schedule, part 1F, the Employer is entitled to deduct from payment to the Contractor the amount stated in the Schedule, part 1F until the collateral warranty is given.

11.4.2 If the Contractor has not submitted a programme or given a progress report when required by sub-clauses 4.9 and 4.10, the Employer is entitled to deduct 15% of each payment to the Contractor until the programme or report has been submitted or given.

11.4.3 If the Contractor has not complied with sub-clause 5.3, the Employer is entitled to make the deduction provided for in sub-clause 5.3.6.

11.4.4 If the Contractor does not give the certificate required by sub-clause 5.3.7 with an interim statement, there shall be no payment due under sub-clause 11.1 for the relevant Work Item until the certificate is given.

11.4.5 Deductions from payments because of obligations that the Contractor has still not complied with by the date the Defects Certificate was issued shall be deducted from the Contract Sum. In the case of a deduction from the Contract Sum because of failure to give the certificate required by sub-clause 5.3.7, the amount deducted shall be the portion of the Contract value of the relevant Work Item that the Employer determines to be the labour portion. The Contractor shall give the Employer any information the Employer requires for this determination.

NOTE

Full payment is dependent on:

(i)   the Contractor has provided all the collateral warranties, otherwise the Employer may deduct the amount stated in Part 1 F of the Schedule;

(ii) the Contractor submitting a programme or a revised programme or progress report otherwise the Employer may deduct 15 percent of each payment until the programme and/or reports are submitted;

(iii) the Contractor complying with sub-clause 5.3 (Pay and Conditions of Employment), otherwise the Employer may make the deduction provided for in sub-clause 5.3.6;

(iv) the Contractor providing a certificate as required by sub-clause 5.3.7, otherwise there shall be no payment due for the relevant work item until the certificate is submitted or provided;

(v)   the Contractor complying with all his obligations by the date the defects certificate is issued.

If there is any deduction to the contract sum as a result of the Contractor's failure to provide the certificate required by sub-clause 5.3.7, the amount deducted shall be the labour-element value for the portion of works, as determined by the Employer. The Contractor has to provide the Employer with any information the Employer requires in order to make the determination.

11.5   Final Statement

11.5.1 Within 2 months after Substantial Completion of the Works is certified, the Contractor shall give to the Employer's Representative a final statement. The Contractor shall include in that statement all money that the Contractor considers to be due from the Employer to the Contractor under or in connection with the Contract. The Employer shall have no liability to the Contractor under or in connection with the Contract for any matter not detailed in the final statement, except under the indemnities in the Contract or Compensation Events occurring after Substantial Completion of the Works was certified.

11.5.2 Within 3 months after receipt of the Contractor's final statement, the Employer's Representative shall issue to the Contractor and to the Employer a penultimate payment certificate certifying the amount that, in the Employer's Representative's opinion, will be due from the Employer to the Contractor, less any final retention to be paid after the Defects Certificate is issued, or from the Contractor to the Employer.

11.5.3 As soon as practicable, no more than 3 months, after the Defects Certificate is issued, the Employer's Representative shall issue a final payment certificate certifying the amount that, in the Employer's Representative's opinion, is finally due from the Employer to the Contractor, or from the Contractor to the Employer. The amount in the final payment certificate shall be the same as the amount in the penultimate payment certificate, except for

(1) the final payment of retention and

(2) adjustments to the Contract Sum because of Compensation Events that happen after Substantial Completion of the Works is certified and

(3) amounts owed by the Contractor that were not included in the penultimate certificate [for example, for Defects that the Contractor has not rectified] and

(4) deductions from the Contract Sum under sub-clause 11.4 and

(5) other amounts that, according to the Contract, are to be paid after Substantial Completion of the Works [such as payments for testing after Substantial Completion].

11.5.4 If the penultimate or final payment certificate states that there is a sum owing to the Contractor, the Contractor shall issue an invoice to the Employer for that sum and the Employer shall pay the amount due on the invoice within 15 working days after receiving the invoice. If the penultimate or final payment certificate states that there is a sum owing to the Employer, the Contractor shall pay the amount due within 10 working days of receipt of the Employer's demand for payment. [Payments and certificates, including the penultimate and final payment certificates and the Defects Certificate, will not relieve the Contractor of any obligations, or be evidence of the value of work or that work has been completed satisfactorily].

NOTE

Within two months after substantial completion is certified, the Contractor shall provide a final statement which shall include all money that the Contractor considers due from the Employer. The Employer shall have no liability to the Contractor for any matter not detailed in the final statement except for indemnities or compensation events occurring after substantial completion was certified. This means the Contractor will have to compile the final account as the works are ongoing. The Contractor must ensure that Sub-Contractors also provide details of their accounts diligently to the Contractor for incorporation into the final statement.

The Contractor's final statement must be a comprehensive document that includes all items that the Contractor claims payment for.

Contract Completion	Contractor's Final Statement	Employer's Representative's Penultimate Certificate
1	2 months	3 months or 5 months after Substantial Completion is certified

Five months total, or seven months in the event that the Contractor does not provide a final statement.

The Final Certificate cannot adjust any value(s) contained in the penultimate certificate. Similarly, items for which the Contractor claims payment that were not included in his final statement cannot be included in the final certificate. The onus is on the Contractor to ensure that his final statement is a comprehensive document.

Monies to be paid to the Contractor, as detailed in the penultimate or final certificate, shall become due and be paid by the Employer within 15 working days after receipt by the Employer of the Contractor's invoice.

Monies to be paid by the Contractor to the Employer, as detailed in the penultimate or final certificate, shall be paid by the Contractor within 10 working days of receipt of the Employer's demand.

Payments and certificates (interim payment certificates, penultimate certificates, final certificate and defects certificates) will not be evidence that the works have been carried out satisfactorily or relieve the Contractor of any of his contractual obligations.

Late payments attract interest at the rate provided in the European Communities (Late Payment in Commercial Transactions) Regulations 2002.

11.6   Time for Payment and Interest

11.6.1   When a payment is to be made under the Contract, and no time for payment is stated, the amount due shall be paid within 30 days of receipt of a demand for payment.

11.6.2   Interest shall be added to any payment not made within the time provided in the Contract, from the date the payment was due under the Contract, at the rate provided in the European Communities (Late Payment in Commercial Transactions) Regulations 2002.

11.7   Value Added Tax

11.7.1   The Contract Sum and other amounts in the Contract, unless otherwise stated, exclude VAT.

11.7.2   The Employer shall pay the Contractor (or the Revenue Commissioners when required by Law or their practice) any VAT arising on the supply under the Contract.

11.7.3   The Contractor shall send the Employer, for each payment, an invoice complying with section 17 of the Value-Added Tax Act 1972.

11.8   Withholding Tax

The Employer shall be entitled to make any deduction or withholding on account of tax required by Legal Requirements or the practice of the Revenue Commissioners.

12 TERMINATION

12.1 Termination on Contractor Default

12.1.1 The Employer may, without limiting any other right or remedy, terminate the Contractor's obligation to complete the Works by notice to the Contractor if any of the following occurs:

(1) the Contractor fails to comply with its obligations under the Contract, and, if the failure can be cured, the Employer's Representative has directed the Contractor to put the matter right, and the Contractor has not done so within 14 days after receiving the direction

(2) the Contractor abandons or, except where required or permitted by the Contract, suspends the execution of the Works

(3) the Contractor fails to proceed regularly and diligently with the execution of the Works

(4) the Contractor fails to maintain the required insurances or performance bond

(5) the Starting Date has not occurred or the Contractor has not started to execute the Works on the Site within 6 weeks of the date the Contract requires

(6) any of the Contractor's warranties in sub-clause 2.5 or sub-clause 2.6 are untrue

(7) the Contractor has committed or caused the Employer to commit a serious breach of Legal Requirements concerning the Works

(8) the Contractor or Contractor's Personnel have committed a breach of the Safety, Health and Welfare at Work Act 2005 or any regulations or code of practice made under it concerning the Works

(9) the Contractor has not complied with sub-clauses 5.3.2 or 5.3.3 either

   (a) within 14 days after notice from the Employer requiring a failure to be put right
   or

   (b) persistently

(10) the Contractor has subcontracted all or any part of the Works in breach of the Contract

(11) any of the following **insolvency events** occur:

   (a) a petition for the appointment of a liquidator to the Contractor is presented and is not dismissed within 10 working days of presentation

   (b) any meeting of creditors of the Contractor is convened or held

   (c) any arrangement or composition with or for the benefit of its creditors [including any compromises or arrangements entered into under sections 201 to 204 of the Companies Act 1963] are proposed or entered into by or in respect of the Contractor

   (d) a supervisor, receiver, administrator, administrative receiver, trustee or encumbrancer takes possession of or is appointed over the Contractor or any of its assets, or any distress, execution or other process is levied or enforced, and not discharged within 10 working days, on the Contractor or any of its assets

   (e) the Contractor ceases or threatens to cease carrying on business, or is, or is regarded by law or by a court to be, or declares itself to be, insolvent or unable to pay its debts as they fall due

(f) a petition is presented to appoint an examiner to the Contractor, or an order is made appointing an examiner to the Contractor

(g) the Contractor, being an individual, becomes bankrupt

(h) any event similar to the above insolvency events occurs in respect of the Contractor in any jurisdiction in which it is incorporated or has a place of business

(12) the Contractor, if an individual, dies or becomes incapable of performing the Contract.

12.1.2 If the Contractor is more than one person, if any of the insolvency events occur in respect of any of them, the Employer may either

(1) terminate the Contractor's obligation to complete the Works or

(2) terminate the obligation to complete the Works of the person concerned and the others shall remain liable to perform the Contractor's obligations.

12.1.3 If any insolvency events occur in respect of any person who has guaranteed the Contractor's performance of the Contract to the Employer, or a guarantee ceases to be enforceable against the guarantor, the Employer may terminate the Contractor's obligation to complete the Works unless, within 10 working days of the event, the Contractor has arranged a replacement guarantee and guarantor to the Employer's satisfaction.

NOTE

Grounds for termination by the Employer are:

(i) the Contractor fails to comply with his obligations under the contract;

(ii) the Contractor suspends or abandons the works;

(iii) the Contractor fails to proceed regularly and diligently;

(iv) the Contractor fails to provide the required insurances or performance bond;

(v) the starting date has not occurred or the Contractor has not commenced the works on site within six weeks of the contract date;

(vi) any of the Contractor's warranties in sub-clause 2.5.2 (Safety, Health and Welfare) or sub-clause 2.6 (Ethics in Public Office) are untrue;

(vii) the Contractor committed or caused the Employer to commit a serious breach of legal requirements in relation to the works;

(viii) the Contractor committed a breach of the Safety Health and Welfare at Work Act 2005;

(ix) the Contractor has not complied with sub-clause 5.3.2 or 5.3.3 (Pay and Conditions of Employment);

(x) the Contractor has sub-contracted all or part of the works in breach of the Contract;

(xi) insolvency (eight issues);

(xii) the Contractor, if an individual, dies or becomes incapable of performing the Contract.

12.2   Consequences of Default Termination

If the Contractor's obligation to complete the Works is terminated under sub-clause 12.1, the following shall apply:

12.2.1 The Contractor shall leave the Site in an orderly manner.

12.2.2 Payment of all sums of money that may then be due from the Employer to the Contractor shall be postponed, and the Employer shall not be required to make any further payment to the Contractor except as provided in this sub-clause.

12.2.3 The Employer's Representative shall, as soon as practicable, determine the amount due to the Contractor under the Contract for the Works completed in accordance with the Contract and unpaid (the **termination value**).

12.2.4 The Contractor shall not remove any Works Items or Contractor's Things from the Site unless directed to do so by the Employer, and if directed, shall promptly remove from the Site any Works Items and Contractor's Things, as directed.

12.2.5 The Employer may engage other contractors, use any Works Items and Contractor's Things on the Site and do anything necessary for the completion of the Works.

12.2.6 The Contractor shall, if so directed by the Employer's Representative, assign to the Employer [without further payment] the benefit of any subcontract, contract for the supply of any Works Item, or other contract concerning the Contract.

12.2.7 The Employer may pay to any Subcontractor or supplier to the Contractor any amount due to it that the Employer's Representative certifies as included in any previous interim payment to the Contractor. The Contractor shall re-pay to the Employer such an amount on request.

12.2.8 The Contractor shall give the Employer all Works Requirements and Contractor's Documents it [or Contractor's Personnel] has.

12.2.9 When the Works have been completed and the termination amount as described below has been determined, the Employer's Representative shall give a certificate to the Contractor and the Employer setting out the total of the following (the **termination amount**):

(1) the Employer's additional cost of completing the Works compared with the cost that would have been incurred if the Works had been completed by the Contractor in accordance with the Contract

(2) loss and damage incurred by the Employer as a result of the termination and its cause

(3) amounts due to the Employer by the Contractor under or in connection with the Contract or in connection with the Works.

12.2.10 If the Employer does not begin to put in place arrangements to complete the Works within 6 months after the termination, the Employer's Representative shall issue this certificate as soon as practicable after the end of this 6 month period, based, if necessary, on estimates.

12.2.11 If the termination amount is less than the termination value, the Contractor shall issue an invoice to the Employer for the difference and the Employer shall pay the amount due on the invoice within 15 working days after receiving the invoice. If the termination amount is more than the termination value, the Contractor shall pay the Employer the difference within 10 working days of receiving the Employer's demand for payment.

NOTE

The consequences of default termination are:

(i) the Contractor is obliged to leave the site in an orderly manner;

(ii) payment of any monies due to the Contractor are postponed and the Employer shall not be required to make any further payment to the Contractor, except as provided in clause 12.2;

(iii) the Employer's Representative, as soon as is practicable, make an assessment of the amount due to the Contractor in respect of works completed in accordance with the contract and unpaid. This is the *Termination Value*;

(iv) the Contractor cannot remove any works items or things from the site unless instructed to do so by the Employer;

    (v)   the Employer may engage other Contractors, use any works items and Contractor's things on the site and do any thing necessary for the completion of the works;

    (vi)   if instructed by the Employer's Representative, the Contractor shall assign to the Employer, without further payment, the benefit of any sub-contract, contract for supply, or other contract in relation to the performance of the works;

    (vii)   the Employer may pay to any sub-contractor, or supplier to the Contractor, any amount due to it that the Employer's Representative certifies as included in any previous interim payment. The Contractor shall repay to the Employer such an amount on request;

    (viii)   the Contractor provides to the Employer all work requirements and Contractor's documents;

    (ix)   when the Works have been completed and the *Termination Amount* has been assessed, the Employer's Representative shall certify the termination amount setting out:

        (a)   the Employer's additional cost of completing the works compared with the cost that would have been incurred if the works had been completed by the Contractor;

        (b)   loss and damage incurred by the Employer as a result of the termination and its cause;

        (c)   amounts due to the Employer by the Contractor.

    (x)   if the Employer does not begin to put in place arrangements for the completion of the works within six months of the termination, the Employer's Representative shall issue the certificate as soon as possible, after the end of the six-month period based, where necessary, on estimates. If the *termination amount* is less than the *termination value* the Contractor shall raise an invoice for the difference and the Employer shall pay that amount within 15 days of receipt of the invoice. If the *termination amount* is more than the *termination value* the Contractor shall pay to the Employer the difference within 10 working days of receiving the Employer's demand for payment.

12.3   Suspension by the Contractor

If the Employer fails to pay any amount due under a certificate issued by the Employer's Representative under the Contract, the Contractor may make of the Employer a written demand for payment, and if the payment has not been made within 15 working days of the receipt of the demand, the Contractor may, on giving notice to the Employer, suspend execution of the Works until the amount has been paid. On receiving the payment, the Contractor shall resume execution of the Works.

NOTE

If the Employer fails to make payment under a payment certificate the Contractor shall make a written demand for payment to the Employer. If the payment is not made within a further 15 working days of the receipt of the demand, the Contractor may, on written notice to the Employer, suspend the works until payment is received. Upon receipt of payment the Contractor shall resume execution of the works.

12.4   Termination by the Contractor

The Contractor shall be entitled to terminate the Contractor's obligation to complete the Works by notice to the Employer if any of the following occur:

    (1)   the Contractor has suspended the execution of the Works for 15 working days in accordance with sub-clause 12.3, and the Employer has still not paid

(2) work has been suspended by direction of the Employer's Representative under sub-clause 9.2 and a right to terminate has arisen under that sub-clause

(3) the execution of the Works or a substantial part of the Works has been suspended for a period of at least 3 months as a consequence of loss or damage that is at the Employer's risk under sub-clause 3.1

(4) an event or circumstance outside the control of the parties makes it physically impossible or contrary to Law for the Contractor to fulfil its obligations under the Contract for a period of at least 6 months.

NOTE

The Contractor may terminate by notice to the Employer if:

(i) the Contractor has suspended the works for 15 working days in accordance with sub-clause 12.3 (Suspension by the Contractor) and the payment has not been made;

(ii) work has been suspended under an instruction by the Employer's Representative under sub-clause 9.2 (Suspension) and a right to terminate has arisen under that sub-clause;

(iii) work or a substantial part of it has been suspended for a period at least three months as a consequence of loss or damage that is at the Employer's risk;

(iv) an event occurs that is outside the control of the parties and that makes it physically impossible or contrary to law for the Contractor to fulfil his obligations for a period of at least six months.

12.5 Termination at Employer's Election

12.5.1 The Employer shall be entitled to terminate the Contractor's obligation to complete the Works at its election on 20 working days notice to the Contractor.

12.5.2 The Employer may not terminate the Contractor's obligation to complete the Works under this sub-clause 12.5 for the purpose of retaining another contractor to execute the Works.

12.5.3 The Employer shall return any performance bond required under this Contract to the Contractor on termination under this sub-clause 12.5.

NOTE

The Employer is entitled to terminate the Contract upon 20 days notice to the Contractor. The Employer cannot engage another Contractor to complete the works. The Employer must return the performance bond to the Contractor.

12.6 Consequences of Termination by Contractor or at Employer's Election

If the Contractor's obligation to complete the Works is terminated under sub-clause 12.4 or sub-clause 12.5 the following shall apply:

12.6.1 The Contractor shall leave the Site in an orderly manner and remove any Contractor's Things.

12.6.2 The Contractor shall give the Employer all Works Requirements and all Contractor's Documents.

12.6.3 The Contractor shall, as soon as practicable, give the Employer's Representative a statement of the total of the following (the **termination sum**):

(1) the unpaid value of the parts of the Works completed to the date of termination in accordance with the Pricing Document, disregarding any provision limiting the Employer's obligation to pay for partially completed work

(2)   the Contractor's reasonable costs of removal from the Site as a consequence of the termination

(3)   all other amounts due to the Contractor under the Contract but not damages.

12.6.4   Within 10 working days of receiving this statement, the Employer's Representative shall issue a certificate to the Contractor and the Employer of the amount due from the Contractor to the Employer or the Employer to the Contractor, including the termination sum in the calculation of the amount due from the Employer to the Contractor. If the certificate shows an amount owing to the Contractor, the Contractor shall issue an invoice to the Employer for that amount, and the Employer shall pay the amount due on the invoice within 15 working days after receiving the invoice. If the certificate shows an amount due to the Employer, the Contractor shall pay the amount due within 10 working days of receiving the Employer's demand for payment.

> **NOTE**
>
> The following shall apply as a consequence of termination by Contractor or at Employer's election:
>
> (i)   the Contractor shall as soon as practicable provide the Employer's Representative with a statement of the following (the *Termination Sum*):
>
>   (a)   the unpaid value of the Works completed to the date of the termination;
>
>   (b)   the Contractor's reasonable costs of removal from site as a result of the termination;
>
>   (c)   all other amounts to which the Contractor is entitled under the contract.
>
> (ii)   Within 10 working days of the receipt of the statement the Employer's Representative shall issue a certificate indicating the amount due from the Contractor to the Employer, or the amount from the Employer to the Contractor. The Contractor shall issue an invoice to the Employer and the Employer shall pay the Contractor within 15 working days of receipt of the invoice. In the event of an amount due to the Employer the Contractor shall pay that amount within 10 working days of receiving the Employer's demand;
>
> (iii)   After termination of the contract the Contractor's obligations survive;
>
> (iv)   The Employer's liability to the Contractor is limited to the amount payable under clause 12 and any other amount that fell due under the Contract before the termination.

12.7   Survival

Termination of the Contractor's obligation to complete the Works shall not affect the Contractor's obligations under the Contract, other than the obligation to complete the Works. [In particular the following provisions of the Contract continue to have effect after termination: sub-clauses 1.1, 1.2, 1.3, 1.4, 1.7, 1.8, 1.9, 2.1, 2.6, 3.4, 3.5, 4.16, 4.17, clause 6, this clause 12 and clause 13.]

12.8   Payment

On termination of the Contractor's obligation to complete the Works, the Employer's liability to the Contractor under or in connection with the Contract shall be limited to payment of the amount provided for in this clause 12, and any other amount that fell due under the Contract before the termination.

12.9   Reference to Conciliation

12.9.1   The Employer may [but is not required to] refer to conciliation under sub-clause 13.1 the issue of whether the Employer has become entitled to terminate the Contractor's obligation to complete the Works under sub-clause 12.1.

12.9.2   Sub-clause 13.1 shall apply to the conciliation, except that the conciliator's time to give the recommendation shall be 21 days after appointment. Clause 13.5 shall also apply.

12.9.3   If the conciliator recommends that the Employer is entitled to terminate the Contractor's obligation to complete the Works under sub-clause 12.1, and the Employer does so within 63 days after receiving the conciliator's recommendation, and it is subsequently found that the Employer was not entitled to do so, then the following shall apply:

(1)   the termination shall stand [even if the circumstances have changed] and have effect as if the Employer's termination notice under sub-clause 12.1 was a valid termination notice under sub-clause 12.5.1

(2)   sub-clauses 12.6.1 to 12.6.4 inclusive shall apply retrospectively from the date of the termination notice under sub-clause 12.1

(3)   sub-clause 12.5.2 shall not apply

(4)   the Contractor shall have no other rights or remedies under the Contract or otherwise at law for the termination.

NOTE

The Employer may refer to conciliation the issue of whether the Employer has become entitled to terminate the Contractor's obligations. The Conciliator's time to give his recommendation is 21 days after his appointment. If it was subsequently found that the Employer was not entitled to terminate the Contractor's obligations then:

(i)   the termination shall stand;

(ii)   sub-clauses 12.6.1 to 12.6.4 (Consequences of Termination by Contractor or at Employer's Election) shall apply retrospectively from the date of the termination notice;

(iii) sub-clause 12.5.2 shall not apply;

(iv)   the Contractor shall have no other rights or remedies under the contract or otherwise at law.

If the Conciliator agrees that a termination breach has occurred, the Employer decides whether or not he will act on that determination. If the Employer decides to terminate and an Arbitrator subsequently finds that the decision to terminate was incorrect, the rights of the Contractor are restricted to the rights the Contractor would have had if the Contract had been terminated at the election of the Employer, ie, value of works to date and reasonable demobilisation costs.

13 DISPUTES

13.1 Conciliation

13.1.1 If a dispute arises under the Contract, either party may, by notice to the other, refer the dispute for conciliation under this sub-clause 13.1. The notice shall state that it is given under sub-clause 13.1 of the Contract.

13.1.2 Within 10 working days of the referral of a dispute to conciliation, the parties shall jointly appoint a conciliator who is competent to adjudicate upon the dispute and independent of the parties. If the parties fail to appoint a conciliator within 10 working days of the referral, or if a person appointed refuses to act or becomes unable to act, the conciliator shall be appointed by the appointing body or person named in the Schedule, part 1N, on the application of either party. If there is a fee for making the appointment, the parties shall share it equally. If one party pays the entire fee, it shall be entitled to reimbursement of the other party's share from the other party on demand.

13.1.3 Each party shall, within the period set by the conciliator, send to the conciliator and the other party brief details of the dispute stating its contentions as to the facts and the parties' rights and obligations concerning the dispute. The conciliator may, for this purpose, suggest further actions or investigations that may be of assistance.

13.1.4 The parties shall promptly make available to the conciliator all information, documents, access to the Site and appropriate facilities that the conciliator requires to resolve the dispute.

13.1.5 The conciliator shall consult with the parties in an attempt to resolve the dispute by agreement. The conciliator may do any of the following, or any combination of them:

(1) meet the parties separately from each other or together and consider documents from one party not sent or shown to the other

(2) conduct investigations in the absence of the parties

(3) make use of specialist knowledge

(4) obtain technical or legal advice

(5) establish the procedures to be followed in the conciliation

13.1.6 The conciliator shall not be an arbitrator and the Arbitration Acts 1954 to 1998 and the law relating to arbitration shall not apply to the conciliation.

13.1.7 The conciliator's terms of appointment shall be those in the Works Requirements or, if there are none, those agreed by the Employer and the Contractor with the conciliator.

13.1.8 If the dispute is not resolved by agreement within 42 days after the conciliator was appointed, or a longer period proposed by the conciliator and agreed by the parties, the conciliator shall give both parties a written recommendation. The conciliator shall base the recommendation on the parties' rights and obligations under the Contract.

13.1.9 If either party is dissatisfied with the conciliator's recommendation, it may, within 42 days after receiving the conciliator's recommendation, so notify the other party. The notice shall state that it is given under sub-clause 13.1 of the Contract, and shall state the matters in dispute and the reasons for dissatisfaction. If the conciliator has failed to give a recommendation within 42 days after appointment, either party may give a notice of dissatisfaction. If notice of dissatisfaction has been given in accordance with this clause, either party may refer the dispute to arbitration under sub-clause 13.2.

13.1.10 If neither party gives notice of dissatisfaction within 42 days after receiving the conciliator's recommendation, the recommendation shall be conclusive and binding on the parties, and the parties agree to comply with it. If, in such circumstances, a party fails to comply with the conciliator's recommendation, the other party may [without limiting its other rights] refer the failure itself to arbitration under sub-clause 13.2, and need not invoke this sub-clause 13.1 for this reference.

13.1.11   If the conciliator has recommended the payment of money and a notice of dissatisfaction is given, the following shall apply:

(1)   The party concerned shall make the payment recommended by the conciliator, provided that the other party first

(a)   gave a notice, complying with the arbitration rules referred to in sub-clause 13.2, referring the same dispute to arbitration and

(b)   gave the paying party a bond executed by a surety approved by the paying party, acting reasonably, in the form included in the Works Requirements, or if there is none, a form approved by the paying party, acting reasonably, for the amount of the payment.

(2)   If, when the dispute is finally resolved, it is found that the party receiving payment on the conciliator's recommendation was not entitled to some or all of the amount paid, then that party shall repay the amount it was paid and found not to be entitled to, together with interest.

(3)   When the dispute is finally resolved, interest will be deducted from final payment under the award or judgment.

(4)   Interest under this sub-clause is calculated at the reference rate referred to in the European Communities (Late Payment in Commercial Transactions) Regulations 2002 plus 2% per year and runs from the date of the original payment to the date of the repayment or final payment.

(5)   [This provision for interest is confidential under sub-clause 13.1.12, and in particular shall not be taken into account or referred to in arbitration until all other matters are resolved.]

13.1.12   The conciliation shall be confidential, and the parties shall respect its confidentiality, except when any of the exceptions in sub-clause 4.16 apply, or to the extent necessary to enforce a recommendation that has become conclusive and binding. All documents provided by a party in connection with a conciliation shall be returned when the conciliation is concluded.

13.2   Arbitration

Any dispute that, under sub-clause 13.1, may be referred to conciliation shall, subject to sub-clause 13.1 be finally settled by arbitration in accordance with the arbitration rules identified in the Schedule, part 1N. For purposes of those rules, the person or body to appoint the arbitrator, if not agreed by the parties, is named in the Schedule, part 1N.

13.3   Jurisdiction

Subject to the above provisions of this clause, the parties submit to the jurisdiction of the Irish courts to settle any dispute that may arise out of or in connection with the Contract or the Works.

13.4   Agent for Service

If an agent for service of legal proceedings on the Contractor is named in part 2A of the Schedule, the Contractor confirms to the Employer that it has irrevocably appointed the named person as its agent for the service of all documents relating to legal proceedings, and that failure of the agent to notify the Contractor of receipt of a document will not invalidate any proceedings or the service of the document.

13.5　Continuing Obligations

[Despite the existence of a dispute, the parties shall continue to perform their obligations under the Contract.]

GENERAL COMMENTS ON SECTION

Any dispute can be referred to conciliation during the course of the Contract. The appointing body for the Conciliator shall be described in the Schedule, Part 1, Section N. If the dispute is not resolved within 42 days after the appointment of the Conciliator, the Conciliator shall make his recommendation. The parties have 45 days to accept the recommendation.

If the recommendation stated that a sum of money should be paid by one party to the other, then that shall be binding in the interim. The receiving party will have to provide a bond for the amount it receives.

If the recommendation is rejected by either party the matter can be referred to arbitration.

Any dispute referred to arbitration shall be subject to the arbitration rules stated in the Schedule, Part I, Section N.

End of Conditions.

CLAUSE PV1 – PRICE VARIATION

PV1.1 Contract Sum Adjustment

The Contract Sum is adjusted for fluctuations in costs of resources only in respect of increases or decreases that occur in workers' wages or expenses, or material prices, or are made by Law, as follows:

PV1.1.1 **Timing:**

    (a) The **Base Date** means the first day of the 31st month after the Contract Date.

    (b) No increase or decrease that comes into being after the Date for Substantial Completion shall be taken into account for the purpose of this clause PV1.

PV1.1.2 **Workers' wages and expenses**

The Contract Sum shall be adjusted by the amount of an increase or decrease in workers' wages or expenses that satisfies all these requirements:

    (i) it is made to the standard normal and overtime hourly wage rates or expenses payable to workers according to the Labour Court's Registered Employment Agreement dated 15 March 1967 as varied from time to time under Section 28 of the Industrial Relations Act 1946 and

    (ii) it becomes payable after the Base Date in accordance with that agreement and

    (iii) it is in respect of General Round Increases conforming to the guidelines of the Social Partnership Agreements between the government, employer organisations and trade unions relating to such increases, or, in the absence of a Social Partnership Agreement and guidelines, increases in accordance with the guidelines on General Round Increases issued by the Department of Finance and

    (iv) the workers in respect of whom an increase is being claimed have received in Ireland for the relevant work at least the increased standard wage rates and expenses.

Workers means

    (a) craftspersons and

    (b) semi-skilled and unskilled labour and

    (c) drivers and operators of plant and machinery and

    (d) time-keepers and clerical staff stationed on site and

    (e) any foreperson, charge hand or other person who supervises or administers while performing duties within (a) – (c), but in respect only of the standard wage rates according to sub-clause PV1.1.2(i) and expenses applicable to those duties and 50% of their total hours worked. [Site agents, managers, other full time supervisors and administrators, and surveyors, for example, are excluded.]

General Round Increases means increases in workers' wages to the extent that they apply generally in the construction industry and are compliant with Government guidelines and Social Partnership Agreements.

Expenses means expenses payable for country money and PRSI payable by the Contractor as employer. [All other increases are excluded, even where calculated as a percentage of a standard rate. So, for example, the Contractor is not entitled to any payment for local or site bargaining provisions; any parity or restructuring increases; any bonus under a site agreement, productivity, incentive, or other bonus; insurance premiums, other on-costs or consequential costs].

PV1.1.3 **Materials**

The Contract Sum shall be adjusted by the amount of an increase or decrease in the Price of material that results from either or both of these calculations where applicable:

- So far as the Price of any material at the Purchase Date has increased by more than 50 percent of the Price at the first business day of the month in which the purchase occurred or the Price at the Designated Date (whichever is highest) then that excess percentage over 50 percent is applied to its Price at the Designated Date.

- So far as the Price of any material at the Base Date has increased or decreased at the Purchase Date by more than 10 percent, then that excess percentage over 10 percent is applied to the Price at the Base Date.

Material means only

(a)   material invoiced to the project

(b)   for incorporation in the permanent Works [as fixtures or unfixed goods],

(c)   or for temporary works used on the Site

(d)   and not used on any previous project or usable on any subsequent one [for example, replaceable components in formwork]. [Tools or equipment are not 'material'. There is no deduction of normal wastage from the allowable quantity of material, or of extra or surplus material taken over by the Employer].

Purchase Date means the date when the particular material was invoiced to the project.

Price means the average price at which the relevant volume of the relevant material is available in the market at the relevant time from a representative number of reputable manufacturers or suppliers. [There is no adjustment for any alteration in the price of material except as specified in this sub-clause].

PV1.1.4 **Law**

The Contract Sum shall be adjusted by the amount of any increase or decrease in the Contractor's cost of performing its obligations under the Contract as a result of a change in Law made after the Designated Date that

(i)   changes [whether by alteration, addition or removal] VAT, excise duty or tariff, requirements for a licence to import or export any Commodity or Pay-Related Social Insurance and

(ii)   is not identified in the Works Requirements and

(iii)   has not resulted in an adjustment in the Contract Sum under another part of this clause PV1 or the Contract.

PV1.2 Communications

The Contractor shall maintain arrangements to become aware of any significant possibility of an increase or decrease in the Contract Sum that may arise in accordance with this clause PV1 and shall immediately notify the Employer's Representative of any such possibility and keep him informed of any opportunities to minimise an increase.

PV1.3 Compensation Events

The Pricing Document and the valuation rules in sub-clause 10.6 shall not cease to determine, apply to or be the basis of the valuation of a Compensation Event by reason of price fluctuations in material costs, but the following principles shall apply:

(i)   No departure from rates in the Pricing Document shall be made in respect of fluctuations affecting the cost of material omitted by a Change Order.

(ii) Valuation of a Change Order shall include any increase in the cost to the Contractor of material substituted or added by the Change Order that is due to price fluctuation after the Designated Date so far as it is likely to exceed the price fluctuation increase that under this clause PV1 would have been the Contractor's risk for the original material. No adjustment under this clause PV1 shall apply to an adjustment or the part of an adjustment of the Contract Sum valued under sub-clauses 10.6.4 or 10.7.

PV1.4 Efficiency

[In addition to sub-clause PV1.1.1(b),] increases of the Contract Sum will only apply so far as the increased costs incurred by the Contractor occur despite its efficient progress and procurement and reasonable efforts to minimise increases.

PV1.5 Certificates & Payment

The Contractor shall fully detail and vouch any fluctuations in costs relevant to this clause PV1 as soon as practicable, and they shall then be allowed for in interim and final certificates and payments under and subject to clause 11.

NOTE

The contract sum is adjusted for fluctuations in costs of resources only in respect of increases or decreases that occur in Workers' wages or expenses, or material prices, or that are made by law. The "base date" means the first day of the 31st month after the contract date. The "contract date" is the date the employer issued the letter of acceptance.

No increase or decrease that comes into being after the date for substantial completion shall be taken into account for the purpose of this clause PV1.

Workers' Wages or Expenses

The contract sum shall be adjusted by the amount of an increase or decrease in workers' wages or expenses that satisfies all these requirements:

(i)   it is made to the standard normal and overtime hourly wage rates or expenses payable to workers according to the Labour Court's Registered Employment Agreement dated 15 March 1967, as varied from time to time under section 28 of the Industrial Relations Act 1946; and

(ii) it becomes payable *after the Base Date* in accordance with that agreement; and

(iii) it is in respect of "general round increases" conforming to the guidelines of the Social Partnership Agreements between the Government, Employer organisations and Trade Unions relating to such increases, or, in the absence of a Social Partnership Agreement and guidelines, increases in accordance with the guidelines on general round increases issued by the Department of Finance; and

(iv) the workers, in respect of whom an increase is being claimed, have received in Ireland for the relevant work at least the increased standard wage rates and expenses.

Materials

The contract sum shall be adjusted by the amount of an increase or decrease in the price of material that results from either or both of these calculations where applicable:

(i)   so far as the price of any material at the purchase date has increased by *more than 50 percent* of the price at the first business day of the month in which the purchase occurred, or the price at the designated date (whichever is highest), then that *excess percentage over 50 percent is applied to its price at the designated date*. The "designated date" is the date 10 days before the last day for receipt of the Contractor's tender for the works, or, if there was none, 10 days before the Employer received the Contractor's tender for the works.

(ii) so far as the price of any material at the base date has increased or decreased at the purchase date by *more than 10 percent*, then that *excess percentage over 10 percent is applied* to the price at the base date.

Certificates and Payment

The Contractor shall fully detail and vouch any fluctuations in costs relevant to this clause PV1 as soon as practicable. The fluctuations shall then be allowed for in interim and final certificates and payments under and subject to clause 11 (Payment).

SCHEDULE

PART 1
(Completed by the Employer before Tender)

A Employer's Representative and Communications
Sub-clauses 4.3 and 4.14

Details for sending notices under clauses 12 and 13 to the Employer are:

For the attention of: ....

Address:

....

....

....

Details for sending other notices and communications to the Employer are:

For the attention of: ....

Address:

....

....

....

Fax: ....

eMail: ....

The Employer's Representative is: ....

Details for sending notices and other communications to the Employer's Representative are:

For the attention of: ....

Address:

....

....

....

Fax: ....

eMail: ....

Limitations on the Employer's Representative's authority to perform its functions and powers under the Contract

- Maximum adjustment to the Contract Sum for a single Change Order: €_____ unless approved by the Employer.

- Maximum cumulative value of adjustments to the Contract Sum for Change Orders in any 3-month period: €_____, unless approved by the Employer.

- The Employer's Representative shall not make a Change Order causing or contributing to a reduction in safety, scope, quality or usefulness of the Works without the Employer's approval

- The Employer must agree to reduce retention if the Defects Period is extended

- The Employer's Representative is to consult with the Employer in relation to any adjustment to the Contract Sum before determining the adjustment

- Where the Employer has appointed a quantity surveyor, the Employer's Representative is to consult with the quantity surveyor in relation to any adjustments to the Contract Sum before determining the adjustment

- ....

- ....

NOTE

Part A provides details for communications with the Employer for notices in connection with clauses 12 (Termination) and 13 (Disputes). This part also provides the name and address of the Employer's Representative and limitations of the Employer's Representative. The limitations are:

    (i)   a maximum value of a change order, unless approved by the Employer;

    (ii)   a maximum number of change orders in any three-month period with a cumulative value of € (to be stated), unless approved by the Employer;

    (iii)   a change order shall not cause or contribute to any reduction in safety, scope, quality or usefulness of the works without the approval of the Employer;

    (iv)   the Employer's Representative must consult the Employer before determining any adjustment to the contract sum;

    (v)   where a quantity surveyor is appointed, the Employer's Representative will consult the quantity surveyor before determining any adjustment to the contract sum;

    (vi)   other limitations may be specified by the Employer.

B   Documents

The **Works Requirements** are:

....

....

....

....

The **Pricing Document** is:

....

....

....

....

The **Works Proposals** are:

....

....

....

NOTE

Part B will contain details of the works requirements, as set out by the Employer, the pricing document and, if there is a bill of quantities, the method of measurement under which the bills were prepared.

C   Project Supervisor
Sub-clause 2.4

The Contractor, or an individual or body corporate named in the Work Proposals, is to be appointed project supervisor for the construction stage for the Works and any other work on the Site between the Starting Date and the date of Substantial Completion of the Works contemplated in the Works Requirements.

NOTE

Part C provides for the appointment of the project supervisor, in accordance with clause 2.4 of the contract. The project supervisor has to be appointed before the starting date. The "starting date" is the day the Contractor proposes to start executing the works, as notified by the Contractor to the Employer's Representative under sub-clause 9.1. If a Contractor takes on this role and fails to adequately perform, resource and provide the necessary insurances the Employer may terminate the Contractor's role and appoint another party to carry out the duties of project supervisor (construction stage). In this event the contractor is replaced in this role and the Contractor is responsible for all the Employer's costs involved in the new appointment.

D Insurance
Clause 3

Insurance of the Works: minimum amount insured for professional fees: 12½%[7] of the Contract Sum.

- Minimum indemnity limit for Public liability insurance: €6,500,000[8] for any one event, but this limit may be on an annual aggregate basis for products liability, collapse, vibration, subsidence, removal and weakening of supports and sudden and accidental pollution.

- Minimum indemnity limit for Employers' liability insurance: €13,000,000[9] for any one event.

- Maximum excess for Insurance of Works and other Risk Items: €10,000[10].

- Maximum excess for Public liability: €10,000[11] in respect of property damage only. There shall be no excess for death, injury or illness.

- No excess for Employers' liability.

Permitted exclusions from the Insurances:

- War, invasion, act of foreign enemies, hostilities [whether war is declared or not], civil war, rebellion, revolution, insurrection or military or usurped power

- Pressure waves caused by aircraft or other airborne objects travelling at sonic or supersonic speeds

- Contamination by radioactivity or radioactive, toxic, explosive or other hazardous properties of any explosive nuclear assembly or its components, in each case not caused by the Contractor or the Contractor's Personnel

- Terrorism (delete if terrorism insurance is required)

- Asbestos (delete if asbestos insurance is required)

Permitted exclusions from insurance of the Works and other Risk Items:

- Use or occupation of the Works by the Employer except in connection with the Works

- Unless otherwise specified in the Works Requirements, cost of making good defects in the Works but not damage caused by such defects to other sound parts of the Works

- Wear, tear, normal upkeep or normal repair or gradual deterioration

- Inventory losses

- Loss of use or any consequential loss of any nature including penalties for delay, non-completion or noncompliance

- Failure of information technology

---

[7] If no percentage stated, 12½% applies.
[8] If no amount stated, €6,500,000 applies.
[9] If no amount stated, €13,000,000 applies.
[10] If no amount stated, €10,000 applies.
[11] If no amount stated, €10,000 applies.

- Mechanical or electrical breakdown but not resulting damage
- Cessation of the Works for more than 3 months

Permitted exclusions from employer's liability insurance:

- Persons under a contract of service or apprenticeship with the insured
- Property of the insured or in the insured's custody or control other than existing premises and their contents temporarily occupied for the purposes of the Works
- Defective workmanship or materials but not resulting damage
- Mechanically propelled vehicles within the meaning of the Road Traffic Acts
- Loss or damage due to design / Design for a fee / Defective workmanship, materials or design but including its consequences (Delete two. If two not deleted, permitted exclusion is 'Loss or Damage due to design'.)
- Gradual pollution or contamination
- Territorial limits
- Unless otherwise specified in the Works Requirements, aircraft and waterborne craft
- Fines, penalties, liquidated damages

Permitted exclusions from employer's liability insurance:

- Offshore work
- Liability compulsorily insurable under the Road Traffic Acts

Permitted exclusions from professional indemnity insurance:

- Persons under a contract of service or apprenticeship with the insured
- Ownership, use, occupation or leasing of mobile or immobile property
- Effecting or maintenance of insurance of or in connection with the provision of finance or advice on financial matters
- Dishonest, malicious, criminal or deliberate illegal acts
- Libel and slander
- Insolvency
- Fines, penalties, liquidated damages or any penal, punitive, exemplary, non-compensatory or aggravated damages
- Failure of information technology
- Contractual liability that would not apply in the absence of the contract

Optional insurance provisions:

The Employer shall not have the risk of loss of and damage to its existing facilities and parts of the Works it uses or occupies, in accordance with sub-clause 3.8.

If Insurance of the Works and other Risk Items is to include terrorism cover, the minimum sum insured shall be € ....

The Contractor is not required to extend the insurance of the Works and other Risk Items for a Section that has reached Substantial Completion until the Employer's Representative issues the certificate of Substantial Completion for the whole Works.

Professional indemnity insurance is not required. If required, the professional indemnity insurance is to be kept in place for _____ years after Substantial Completion of the Works is certified by the Employer's

Representative. If required, the minimum indemnity limit for professional indemnity insurance shall be €_____ for each and every claim or series of claims arising from the same originating cause/annual aggregate limit
(Delete one. If none deleted, read as 'annual aggregate limit'). The maximum excess shall be €50,000[12].

> **NOTE**
>
> Part D deals with insurance requirements for the project. Contractors are familiar with taking out insurances for: all risks; public/products liability; employers' liability; private/commercial motors; professional indemnity; and other ancillary covers. Contractors should advise their insurance company or brokers that they are tendering under the new forms of "Public Works Contract" and provide the insurance company or broker with copies of the required contract insurances. There may be additional insurance premiums to meet the contract requirements. These additional premiums will have to be included in the tender.
>
> It will be necessary for Contractors, when obtaining quotations from Sub-Contractors, to provide the Sub-Contractors with the contract insurance requirements, especially where there is a design element. Sub-Contractors can then incorporate the insurance requirements into their prices for inclusion in the tender. The situation is similar for Sub-Contractors who do not have a design element.

E Performance Bond
Sub-clause 1.5

A performance bond is required.

The amount of the performance bond shall be 25%[13] of the initial Contract Sum up to certification of Substantial Completion of the Works, and 12½%[14] of the initial Contract Sum for the subsequent period stated in the form of bond in the Works Requirements / 450 days after that. (Delete one. If none deleted, read as '450 days after that'.).

> **NOTE**
>
> Part E provides details of the "performance bond" for the project. Every contract is bondable. However, the level of risk undertaken by the Contractor determines the cost of the premium. It is recommended that that the bondsman is provided with a copy of the contract, the schedule and any specific requirements of the tender documents.
>
> Bid bonds may be required, especially where the Contract is subject to EU procurement rules. Bid bonds provide the Employer with a means of security in the event that the successful tenderer refuses to accept the contract, as EU procurement rules do not allow the contract to be awarded to the next unsuccessful tenderer. Bid bonds will be an exception rather than a rule. This again will attract a premium that will have to be included in the tender sum.

F Collateral Warranties
Sub-clause 5.5

Collateral warranties are required from the following categories of Specialists, by the following dates; and the amount withheld from payments under sub-clause 11.4.1 are as follows:

Category of specialist	Date for warranty	Amount withheld	Minimum indemnity limit for professional indemnity insurance	Maximum excess for professional indemnity

---

[12] If no amount stated, €50,000 applies.
[13] If no percentage stated, 25% applies.
[14] If no percentage stated, 12½% applies.

> **NOTE**
>
> Part F provides details of the "collateral warranties" required by the Employer. It is important at tender stage that all Sub-Contractors, designers and professional service contracts (engineering, for example) are provided with a copy of the collateral warranty required of them by the Employer. In the event that a successful tenderer does not provide the required warranties the Employer may withhold monies under clause 11.4.1 of the contract.

G   Dates for Substantial Completion, Sections, Liquidated Damages, Retention (%)

	Date for Substantial Completion	Rate of liquidated damages	Reduction in retention on Substantial Completion of Section
The Works	The Works (Last day of period starting on the Contract Date or date) (unless to be completed by Contractor in part 2)	€.......... per	
Section: (Employer to complete names of sections)		€.......... per	
Section: (Employer to complete names of sections)		€.......... per	
Section: (Employer to complete names of sections)		€.......... per	
Section: (Employer to complete names of sections)		€.......... per	

> **NOTE**
>
> These details will be provided by the Employer.

H   Early Completion
Sub-clause 9.6

The Employer's Representative is required to issue the certificate of Substantial Completion if the Works or a Section reaches Substantial Completion before its Date for Substantial Completion.

> **NOTE**
>
> The Employer can exercise the option of not being obliged to issue a certificate of substantial completion in the event of the Contractor finishing early. In such an event, the works remain the responsibility of the Contractor, to include security, insurances, and maintenance of mechanical and electrical components. The bond would not be released until substantial completion.

I   Defects Period

The initial Defects Period is one year[15] from the date of Substantial Completion of the Works.

---

[15] If no period stated, one year applies.

> **NOTE**
>
> The Employer will specify the defects period.

J Random Checks for Employment Records

Sub-clause 5.3.3A(2) shall be part of the Contract.

> **NOTE**
>
> The Employer can reserve the right to make random checks under sub-clause 5.3.3A(2) to establish that correct rates of pay apply to all operatives engaged on the project.

K Delay Events, Compensation Events, Programme Contingency, Delay Costs, Adjustments
Sub-clauses 9.3, 9.4, 10.1, 10.6, 10.7

Delay Events and Compensation Events are as follows:

Event	Delay Event	Compensation Event
1. The Employer's Representative gives the Contractor a Change Order	Yes	Yes
2. The Employer's Representative directs the Contractor to search for Defects or their cause and no Defect is found, and the search was not required because of a failure of the Contractor to comply with the Contract	Yes	Yes
3. The Employer's Representative directs the Contractor to Suspend work under sub-clause 9.2	Yes	Yes
4. The Contractor suspends work in accordance with subclause 12.3	Yes	Yes
5. There is a factual error in information about the Site or setting out information in the Works Requirements. [This does not include an error of interpretation.]	Yes	Yes
6. (not used)	–	–
7. The Employer's Representative does not give the Contractor an instruction required under sub-clause 4.5.4 within the time required under sub-clause 4.11.2 when the Contractor has asked for the instruction in accordance with sub-clause 4.11.1	Yes	Yes
8. The Employer does not allow the Contractor to occupy and use a part of the Site in accordance with sub-clause 7.1	Yes	Yes
9. The Employer does not give the Contractor a Works Item or other thing as required by the Contract when the Contractor has asked for it in accordance with sub-clause 4.11.1	Yes	Yes
10. Employer's Personnel working on the Site under clause 7.6 interfere with the execution of the Works on the Site, and the interference is unforeseeable and not in accordance with the Contract	Yes	Yes

Event		Delay Event	Compensation Event
11.	The Employer instructs the Contractor under sub-clause 3.2.3 to rectify loss of or damage to Risk Items for which the Contractor is not responsible	Yes	Yes
12.	Loss of or damage to the Works that is at the Contractor's risk in accordance with sub-clause 3.2	Yes	No
13.	A **weather event** as described below	Yes	No
14.	A strike or lockout affecting the construction industry generally or a significant part of it, and not confined to employees of the Contractor or any Contractor's Personnel	Yes	No
15.	Delay to the Works caused by the order or other act of a court or other public authority exercising authority under Law, that did not arise as a result of or in connection with an act, omission or breach of Legal Requirements of the Contractor or the Contractor's Personnel or a breach of the Contract by the Contractor	Yes	No
16.	A breach by the Employer of the Contract delaying the Works that is not listed elsewhere in this table	Yes	Yes
17.	A difference between the Contract value of the Works according to the quantities and descriptions in a Bill of Quantities in the Pricing Document, if there is one, [taking into account the method of measurement and any amendments identified below] and the Contract value of the Works described in the Works Requirements, because the Bill of Quantities, when compared with the Works Requirements • includes an incorrect quantity or • includes an item that should not have been included or • excludes an item that should have been included or • gives an incorrect item description and the difference for an item in, or that should have been in, the Bill of Quantities is more than €500.	No	No
18.	An item of archaeological interest or human remains is found on the Site, and it was unforeseeable	Yes	Yes
19.	The Contractor encounters on the Site unforeseeable ground conditions or unforeseeable human-made obstructions in the ground, other than Utilities	Yes	Yes
20.	The Contractor encounters unforeseeable Utilities in the ground on the Site	Yes	Yes
21.	Owners of Utilities on the Site do not relocate or disconnect Utilities as stated in the Works Requirements, when the Contractor has complied with their procedures and the procedures in the Contract, and the failure is unforeseeable	Yes	Yes

In the above table

Utilit means conducting media and apparatus for water, sewage, electricity, gas, oil, telecommunications, data, am, air, or other services, and associated apparatus and structures.

A condition, circumstance or occurrence is **unforeseeable** if an experienced contractor tendering for the Works could not have reasonably foreseen it on the Designated Date, having inspected the Site and its surroundings and having satisfied itself, insofar as practicable and taking into account any information in connection with the Site provided by the Employer, as to all matters concerning the Site, including its form and nature and its geotechnical, hydrological and climatic conditions.

If there is a Bill of Quantities, the **method of measurement** according to which it was prepared and measurements are to be made is

except when any statement or general or detailed description of the work in the Contract shows the contrary.

A **weather measurement** for a month means

* number of days with rainfall exceeding 10mm

* number of days with minimum air temperature less than 0° Celsius

* number of days with maximum mean 10 minute wind speed exceeding 15 metres per second.

A **weather event** is when a weather measurement is recorded at _____ weather station for a month between the Starting Date and the Date for Substantial Completion of the Works that is shown to exceed the 90th percentile of past weather measurements for the corresponding month of the year at the same station, as determined by Met Éireann and published most recently before the Designated Date.

If no weather station is named above, the Met Éireann station nearest the Site shall be used. If the station named above, or the nearest one, does not make or record a weather measurement, the station nearest to the Site that records the weather measurement shall be used.

A weather event also means the following:

An extension of time for a weather event shall never exceed the number of Site Working Days equal to the number of days in the relevant month by which the weather measurement exceeds the 90th percentile (as so determined and published).

In **sub-clause 9.4** the programme contingency is _____ Site Working Days of delay caused by Compensation Events.

The definition of craftspersons in part 2D (for **sub-clause 10.6.4(1)**) includes the following additional categories:

In **sub-clause 10.6.4(3)**, the rates to be used to determine the cost of plant are the rates in modified as follows:

• Rates will be treated as if in euro

• ....

and any rates in the Pricing Document.

In **sub-clause 10.7**, the amount to be added for delay cost is the daily rate tendered by the Contractor in the Schedule, part 2D (sub-clause 10.7.1(1)) / the expenses unavoidably incurred as a result of the delay (subclause 10.7.1(2)) (Delete as applicable. If neither deleted, expenses unavoidably incurred as a result of the delay to be read as deleted.)

For purposes of sub-clause 10.7, the Contractor is to tender in part 2D a single daily rate for delay costs / separate daily rates for delay costs for each of the following periods or parts of the Works:

• ....

• ....

• ....

(If the above are blank, and sub-clause 10.7.1(1) applies, Contractor is to tender a single daily rate.)

NOTE

Section K of Part 1 of the Schedule is where the Contractor will identify the risks transferred to the Contractor. Sub-clauses 9.3 (Delay and Extension of Time), 9.4 (Programme Contingency), 10.1 (Compensation Event), 10.6 (Adjustments to the Contract Sum) and 10.7 (Delay Cost) apply.

A delay event is when the Contractor becomes aware that work is being, or is likely to be, delayed. From the heading in the contract, this will be at the heart of the contract and will require the Contractor's attention.

There are 21 "delay events" and/or "compensation events" listed. Delay and compensation events are items 1, 2, 3, 4, 5, 6, 7, 8, 9, 10, 11, 16, 18, 19, 20 and 21. Delay-only events are items 12, 13, 14 and 15. The compensation-only event is Item 17, where compensation is electable by the Employer at tender stage. Taking each event in turn:

   1 – *"The Employer's Representative gives the Contractor a Change Order"*: In Section A the limitations placed on the Employer's Representative will be specified. In the event that the Employer's Representative exceeds his powers the Contractor should query the instruction. It is thought at this stage that if the Employer's Representative exceeded his powers the Employer would be bound by the Employer's Representative instruction.

   2 – *"The Employer's Representative directs the Contractor to search for defects or their cause and no defect is found... etc."*: This can be both a delay event and a compensation event similar in terms to the GDLA clause 9 (Works to be Opened Up).

   3 – *"The Employer's Representative directs the Contractor to suspend work under sub-clause 9.2 (Suspension)"*. This is both a delay and compensation event.

   4 – *"The Contractor suspends work in accordance with sub-clause 12.3 (Suspension by Contractor)"*. This is both a delay and compensation event.

   5 – *"There is a factual error in information about the Site or setting out information in the Works Requirements. [This does not include an error of interpretation.]"*: This is both a delay and compensation event. An example of this would be incorrect ordinance survey datum or a part of the site not legally in the possession of the Employer.

   6 – *"The Employer takes over part of the Works before Substantial Completion of the Works and any relevant Section"*. Should the Employer take over any part of the works before the contract date for substantial completion, any resultant delays are delay and compensation events. The Contractor has to consent to partial possession or sectional completion.

7 – *"The Employer's Representative does not give the Contractor an instruction required under sub-clause 4.5.4* [instructions] *within the time under sub-clause 4.11.2* [latest date for Employer's Representative to give required instructions] *when the Contractor has asked for instruction in accordance with sub-clause 4.11.1* [contractor to give at least 10 days' advance notice of the date the instruction is required]": This is both a delay and compensation event.

8 – *"The Employer does not allow the Contractor to occupy and use of a part of the Site in accordance with sub-clause 7.1* [Lands made available for the works]": This is both a delay and compensation event.

9 – *"The Employer does not give the Contractor a Works Item or other thing as required by the Contract when the Contractor has asked for it in accordance with sub-clause 4.11.1"*: This is identical to item 7 above and is both a delay and compensation event.

10 – *"Employer's Personnel working on the Site under clause 7.6 interfere with the execution of the Works on the Site, and the interference is unforeseeable and not in accordance with the Contract"*: This is both a delay and compensation event. In the event that the interference is foreseeable then it is deemed to be included for within the Contractor's tender bid.

11 – *"The Employer instructs the Contractor under sub-clause 3.2.3* [Care Of The Works] *to rectify loss of or damage to Risk Items for which the Contractor is not responsible"*: This is both a delay and compensation event.

The foregoing items are similar to variations occurring in the current standard forms.

The following items are delay-only events:

12 – *"Loss or damage to the Works that is at the Contractor's risk in accordance with sub-clause 3.2* [Care of the Works]": This is the alternative to Item 11 and is a delay-only event.

13 – *"A weather event as described below"*: This is a delay-only event. It is far more restricted than current standard forms and is defined against a parameter set out in the contract which is a 10-year weather event. Rainfall, air temperature and wind speed are measured against records contained in the named weather station or, if a weather station is not named, then the nearest weather station shall be used.

14 – *"A strike or lockout affecting the construction industry generally or a significant part of it, and not confined to employees of the Contractor or any Contractor's Personnel"*: This is a delay-only event. Site-only strikes and lockouts are excluded.

15 – *"Delay to the Works caused by the order or other act of a court or other public authority exercising authority under Law, that did not arise as a result of or in connection with an act, omission or breach of Legal Requirements of the Contractor or the Contractor's Personnel or a breach of the Contract by the Contractor"*. This is a delay-only event. These are beyond either party's control, and are therefore delay only.

Delay and Compensation Event

16 – *"A breach by the Employer of the Contract delaying the Works that is not listed elsewhere in this table"*: This is both a delay and compensation event. This is a catch-all clause which empowers the date for substantial completion to be adjusted for an item that is not already catered for in the contract. This then prevents time becoming "at large".

Compensation Event (Employer Electable)

17 – *"A difference between the Contract value of the Works according to the quantities and descriptions in a Bill of Quantities in the Pricing Document, if there is one,* [taking into account the method of measurement and any amendments identified below] *and the Contract value of the Works described in the Works Requirements, because the Bill of Quantities, when compared with the Works Requirements*

- *includes an incorrect quantity or*

- *includes an item that should not have been included or*

- *excludes an item that should have been included or*

- *gives an incorrect item description*

and the difference for an item in, or that should have been in, the Bill of Quantities is more than €500".

Delay and Compensation Events

18 – *"An item of archaeological interest or human remains is found on the Site, and it was unforeseeable"*: An item of value or archaeological or geological interest or human remains being found on the site, which was unforeseeable, will be a delay event and compensation event. A discovery of these items has to be unforeseeable. So if there is evidence of the existence of such items in Employer's reports/surveys then they are foreseeable. Archaeological items exist in heritage towns, areas of historical interest and the like.

19 – *"The Contractor encounters on the Site unforeseeable ground conditions or man-made obstructions in the ground, other than Utilities".*

20 – *"The Contractor encounters unforeseeable Utilities in the ground on the site"*. Utilities means conducting media and apparatus for water, sewage, electricity, gas, oil, telecommunications, data, steam, air or other services and associated apparatus and structures.

21 – *"Owners of utilities on the Site do not relocate or disconnect Utilities as stated in with the Works Requirements, when the Contractor has complied with their procedures and the procedures in the Contract, and the failure is unforeseeable".*

Sub-clause 9.4 [Programme Contingency] – thresholds. The Employer will state in the tender documents the number of days for the contingency for the threshold to be included within the Contractor's programme. The Contractor will have to include the cost related to the contingency for the threshold within his tender. The threshold will be a number of site working days' delay caused by compensation events for which the Contractor will not receive compensation. If the total number of site working days' delay to substantial completion of the works caused by compensation events (for which the Contractor would otherwise be entitled to an extension) is less than the threshold, there shall be no extensions to the initial date for substantial completion of the works for delay caused by compensation events.

If the total number of site working days' delay to substantial completion of the works caused by compensation events (for which the contractor would otherwise be entitled to an extension) exceeds the programme contingency threshold in the Schedule, Part 1k, the number of site working days stated as that threshold shall be deducted from the total number of site working days' extension to the initial date for substantial completion of the works for delay caused by compensation events.

If a successful tenderer includes contingency delay costs in his tender and the delays do not occur then the Contractor benefits.

L   Payment Particulars
Clause 11

Period for interim payment is monthly[16].

Minimum amount for interim payments, except release of retention, €0.00[17]

Up to the percentage stated below of the Contract value of the following unfixed Works Items may be included in an interim payment in accordance with sub-clause 11.2.

On-Site Materials	% of Contract value
	90

---
[16] If no period stated, monthly applies.
[17] If no amount stated, no minimum applies.

On-Site Materials with Bond	% of Contract value
	90

The retention percentage is 10%[18].

> **NOTE**
>
> This section will specify the periods of payments. It will also specify the minimum amount for interim payments, the percentage of unfixed Works Items that will be paid and the retention percentage to apply.

M   (not used)

N   **Conciliation and Arbitration**
Sub-clauses 13.1.2, 13.2

Failing agreement, the conciliator will be appointed by:

The arbitration rules are the Public Works and Services Arbitration Rules, 2008.

The person or body to appoint the arbitrator, if not agreed by the parties, is:

O   **Rights in Contractor's Documents**
Sub-clause 6.4

Copyright and all other rights in the following Contractor's Documents and Works Proposals described in subclause 6.4.2 transfers to the Employer in accordance with sub-clause 6.4.

---

[18] If no percentage stated, 10% applies.

PART 2
(Completed by the Contractor and included with Tender)

A Communications
Sub-clause 4.14

Details for sending notices under clauses 12 and 13 to the Contractor are:

For the attention of: ....
Address:
....
....
....

Details for sending other notices to the Contractor are:

For the attention of: ....
Address:
....
....
....
Fax: ....
eMail: ....

The Contractor's agent[19] in the Republic of Ireland for service of legal process is:

Name:..
Address:
....
....
....
....

> **NOTE**
>
> The tenderer will provide details of the name and address of the individual within the company who will receive notices from the Employer under clauses 12 (Termination) and 13 (Conciliation and Arbitration). The tenderer will also provide details of names and addresses for the Employer to serve other notices.

B (not used)

C Dates for Substantial Completion

	Date for Substantial Completion Number of days after the Contract Date (To be completed by Contractor in Tender **ONLY** if not completed by Employer in Part 1)
The Works	
Section: (Employer to complete names of sections)	

---

[19] An agent in the State must be named if the Contractor's registered office or other principal place of business is outside the State.

Section: (Employer to complete names of sections)	
Section: (Employer to complete names of sections)	
Section: (Employer to complete names of sections)	

NOTE

The tenderer shall complete the dates for substantial completion if not completed by the Employer in Part 1.

D   Adjustments to the Contract Sum including Delay Costs
Sub-clauses 10.6 *and* 10.7

The Contractor's tendered hourly rates for labour and related costs [including PRSI, benefits, tool money, travelling time and country money]:

* Craftspersons   €............ per hour

* General Operatives   €............ per hour

* Apprentices   €............ per hour

(If left blank, or stated as a negative value, read as zero.)

Craftspersons means those categories of work persons described as 'craftsmen' or 'electricians' in employment agreements registered under the Industrial Relations Acts 1946 to 2004, and, any additional categories listed in part 1K.

General Operatives means all direct labour other than craftspersons and apprentices.

Apprentices means categories of work persons under a contract of apprenticeship for trades whose practitioners fall within the above definition of craftspersons.

The Contractor's tendered percentage addition for costs of materials.................%

The Contractor's tendered percentage addition/deduction for costs of plant.................%

All of the above shall include on-costs, overheads and profit, and exclude VAT.
(If either of the above is left blank, read as zero.)

The Contractor's tendered rate of delay costs is €_____ excluding VAT per Site Working Day. (If left blank, or stated as a negative value, read as zero.)

If part 1K states that separate rates are to be tendered for separate periods or parts of the Works, the Contractor's tendered rates are as follows:

Period or part of the Works (part 1K)	Tendered Rate
o	€............................ per Site Working Day
o	€............................ per Site Working Day
o	€............................ per Site Working Day
o	€............................ per Site Working Day

NOTE

This section will be the most difficult and challenging for Contractors and will play a key role in determining the success of the tender bid.

All-in hourly rates for crafts-persons, general operatives and apprentices will have to be completed. There are no differentiations in the categories of crafts-persons or the grades of apprentices unless stated otherwise in the work requirements. A number of delay hours for operatives will be provided by the Employer.

A percentage addition to the cost of materials will have to be quoted.

A percentage addition to the cost of plant will have to be quoted.

Sub-clause 10.7 of the Schedule requires the Contractor to state the amount per day he will be recompensed for site delays. The figures will also be used by the Employer to establish the most economically advantageous tender.

The Contractor will have to calculate a site daily delay cost which will include his own costs, in addition to sub-contactors' and all other costs. There is no scope for recovering any further additional costs.

The daily amount quoted by the Contractor in the Schedule Part 2E is the amount by which the contract sum will be adjusted for delays arising from delay and compensation events only, regardless of whether or not the Contractor's full costs are covered.

In the event that a Contractor leaves the site daily delay cost blank then the amount is taken as zero.

The Employer may request site daily delay costs for different periods or portions of the works. The Contractor has to quote these rates within his tender.

Most Economically Advantageous Tender

Tenders may be assessed on the basis of the "Most Economically Advantageous Tender". In assessing the tenders on this basis, to achieve the most economically advantageous tender, the Employer will add to the tendered sum for the works the following figures that the Contractor has to quote in his tender:

(i)   The delay days multiplied by the tendered site daily cost;

(ii)   The hours for works persons multiplied by the tendered hourly rates;

(iii)   The tendered percentage addition for materials;

(iv)   The tendered percentage addition for plant;

(v)   VAT as appropriate.

PART II

PUBLIC WORKS CONTRACTS

MODEL FORMS

CONTENTS

1. Form of tender 104

2. Form of bid bond 107

3. Form of letter to apparently unsuccessful tender 108

4. Form of letter of intent 109

5. Form of letter of acceptance 110

6. Form of performance bond 111

7. Form of parent company guarantee 113

8. Form of novation and guarantee deed 116

9. Form of appointment of project supervisor for construction stage only 120

10. Form of appointment of project supervisor for construction stage and design process 122

11. Form of appointment of project supervisor for design process only 124

12. Form of professional indemnity insurance certificate 126

13. Form of collateral warranty 128

14. Form of novation agreement 131

15. Form of rates of pay and conditions of employment certificate 133

16. Form of bond – unfixed works items 134

17. Form of retention bond 136

18. Form of conciliator's agreement 137

19. Form of bond – conciliator's recommendation 139

Text in [Square brackets] identifies items to be filled-in by the Employer when these forms are included in Works Requirements.

MODEL FORM 1

FORM OF TENDER

[*Date*]

To [*Name and address of Employer*]
For the attention of [*contact person identified in tender documents*]

[*Name of Contract*]

A Dhaoine Uaisle

We have examined and understand the [*insert full name of selected contract form*], the Works Requirements, the Pricing Document, [Novated Design Documents] all as amended by any supplemental information, for the above contract. Terms used in this Tender that are defined in those documents have the same meaning in this Tender. We submit with this Tender the completed Pricing Document and Schedule [and Works Proposals listed in the attached Schedule Part 2], which form part of this Tender. [We adopt the Novated Design Documents as our Works Proposals].

We offer to complete the Works on the terms of and in conformity with the documents referred to in the preceding paragraph for the lump sum of ....
.... euro including VAT, as adjusted in accordance with the Contract.

In preparing this Tender we have taken account of the obligations relating to employment protection and working conditions that are in force in the place where the works are to be carried out, including the Contract requirements.

We agree that this offer will remain open for your acceptance at any time until the latest of:

- the end of the period specified in your invitation to tender

- expiry of at least 21 days written notice to terminate this Tender given by us.

Your acceptance of this Tender within that time will result in the Contract being formed between us.

We agree that you are not bound to accept the lowest or any tender you may receive.

Is sinne, le meas

Given under the tenderer's common seal   affix common seal

....

....
(*signatures of persons authorised to authenticate the seal*)

OR Signed, sealed and delivered by
.... (*name of attorney*)
as lawful attorney of the tenderer   ....
under a power of attorney dated ....   (*signature of attorney*)
                                                                            affix attorney's personal seal
in the presence of
.... (*signature of witness*)
.... (*name of witness*)
.... (*witness' occupation*)
.... (*witness' address*)

OR (if the tenderer is an individual)
Signed, sealed and delivered by

.... *(name of tenderer)*

....
(signature of tenderer)
affix Contractor's personal seal

in the presence of

.... *(signature of witness)*
.... *(name of witness)*
.... *(witness' occupation)*
.... *(witness' address)*

Note: If the tenderer is a partnership or joint venture, execution must be by each member, using the blocks below.

Joint venture member 1

Given under the common seal of

.... *(name of joint venture member 1)*

affix common seal

....
....
(signatures of persons authorised to authenticate the seal)

OR **Signed, sealed and delivered** by

.... *(name of attorney)*
as lawful attorney of ....
(name of joint venture member 1)

under a power of attorney dated ....

....
(signature of attorney)
affix attorney's personal seal

in the presence of

.... *(signature of witness)*
.... *(name of witness)*
.... *(witness' occupation)*
.... *(witness' address)*

Joint venture member 2

Given under the common seal of

.... *(name of joint venture member 2)*

affix common seal

....
....
(signatures of persons authorised to authenticate the seal)

OR **Signed, sealed and delivered** by

.... *(name of attorney)*
as lawful attorney of ....
(name of joint venture member 2)

under a power of attorney dated ....

....
(signature of attorney)
affix attorney's personal seal

in the presence of

.... *(signature of witness)*
.... *(name of witness)*
.... *(witness' occupation)*
.... *(witness' address)*

Joint venture member 3

Given under the common seal of

.... *(name of joint venture member 3)*   affix common seal

....

....

(signatures of persons authorised to authenticate the seal)

OR **Signed, sealed and delivered** by

.... *(name of attorney)*

as lawful attorney of ....

(name of joint venture member 3)

under a power of attorney dated ....
in the presence of

....

(signature of attorney)

affix attorney's personal seal

.... *(signature of witness)*
.... *(name of witness)*
.... *(witness' occupation)*
.... *(witness' address)*

SCHEDULE TO BE APPENDED –

PART 1 TO BE COMPLETED BY EMPLOYER IN ISSUED DOCUMENTS

PART 2 TO BE COMPLETED BY TENDERER AND SUBMITTED WITH TENDER]

MODEL FORM 2

FORM OF BID BOND

[*Date*]

To [*Name and address of Employer*]

[*Name of Contract*]

[*Name and address of bidder*] (the **Bidder**) proposes to submit a tender to you for the above contract. It is a requirement for submitting the tender that a bond, in these terms and in the amount of [10]% of the amount of the tendered contract sum, be submitted with the tender.

BY THIS BID BOND, we, ...[*Name and address of Surety*] guarantee to you that, if you accept the bidder's tender, the bidder will, within the time required by the contract formed by that acceptance, execute under seal and deliver the Agreement referred to in that contract and give you the fully executed and delivered performance bond and other documents required under clause 9.1 of the Conditions of that contract, all in compliance with the contract. If the bidder fails to do so, or otherwise repudiates its tender, we will, subject to this bond, pay all the loss you sustain as a result, up to the maximum of €...

This bond will expire on [[120] days after the last date for receipt of tender], when we will be released of liability under it, unless you have before that date notified us that the bidder has defaulted in any of the obligations guaranteed by this bond.

We will not be released in any way or discharged by time, indulgence, waiver, alteration, release or compromise or any other circumstances that might operate as a release of a guarantor at law or in equity.

This bond is governed by and construed according to Irish law and we submit to the jurisdiction of the Irish courts to determine all matters concerning it.

We appoint .... of .... as our agent for the service of legal proceedings. We confirm that the named agent has been irrevocably appointed and the agent's failure to notify us of receipt of a document will not invalidate any proceedings or the service of the document.[20]

Given under our common seal

---

[20] An address in Ireland is required when the Surety does not have a registered office in Ireland.

MODEL FORM 3

FORM OF LETTER TO APPARENTLY UNSUCCESSFUL TENDERERS

[*Date*]

To [*Name and address of unsuccessful tenderer*]

[*Name of Contract*]

A Dhaoine Uaisle

I write to inform you that we have assessed the tenders received for the above contract and have determined that the most economically advantageous tender was submitted by.............................

It is our intention [subject to the approval of [*funding department*]] to enter into the contract with that tenderer. It is anticipated that a letter of acceptance will issue to them not earlier than [14] days from the date of this letter.

I would like to thank you for the interest you have shown in this competition.

Please acknowledge receipt of this letter.

Is mise, le meas

Signed: ....
On behalf of the Employer

MODEL FORM 4

FORM OF LETTER OF INTENT

[*Date*]

To [*Name and address of bidder*]

[*Name of Contract*]

Subject to Contract/Contract Denied

A Dhaoine Uaisle

I refer to your tender for the above contract.

I write to inform you that we intend to issue a Letter of Acceptance to you within 14 days after receiving the following items:

- Performance Bond in the form included in the Works Requirements

- evidence of the insurances required by the contract

- Tax Clearance Certificate

- [*add any other conditions, e.g. funding approval, manager's order, board approval, parent company guarantee, collateral warranties*]

If any of the above listed items are not provided within [•] days of the date of this letter, we may proceed to award the Contract to another tenderer.

This is not the Letter of Acceptance. The Employer has not accepted your tender.

Please return a copy of this letter acknowledging receipt as indicated below.

Is mise, le meas

Signed: ....
On behalf of the Employer

We acknowledge receipt of this letter on ....

Signed: ....
On behalf of the Contractor

MODEL FORM 5

FORM OF LETTER OF ACCEPTANCE

[*Date*]

To [*Name and address of Contractor*]

[*Name of Contract*]

A Dhaoine Uaisle

I refer to your tender for the above Contract dated .... (the **Tender**). Terms used in this letter that are defined in the Conditions of that Contract have the same meaning in this letter.

I write to inform you that [*name of Employer*] accepts the Tender. This is the Letter of Acceptance referred to in the Conditions.

The contract formed by this acceptance consists of the following documents:

- This Letter of Acceptance
- The Agreement
- The Conditions of [*insert full name of the selected form of public works contract*]
- The Schedule appended to this Letter of Acceptance
- The Works Requirements identified in the Schedule
- The Pricing Documents identified in the Schedule
- The Works Proposals identified in the Schedule (including any Novated Design Documents identified in the Schedule)
- The following post-tender clarifications:
  ....
  ....
  ....
  ....

The Contract Sum is...euro, including VAT.

I draw attention to your obligations in clause 9.1 of the conditions about documents to be provided before the Starting Date.

Please return to me a copy of this letter acknowledging receipt as indicated below.

Is mise, le meas

Signed: ....
On behalf of the Employer
Duly authorised to accept the Tender

We acknowledge receipt of this letter on ....

Signed: ....
On behalf of the Contractor

SCHEDULE TO BE APPENDED

MODEL FORM 6

FORM OF PERFORMANCE BOND
(Clause 1.5)

Bond No ....
BOND AMOUNT: €..

THIS BOND (the Bond) is made on ....

BETWEEN

1. ....
    whose registered office is at .... (the **Contractor**)
2. ....
    whose registered office is at .... (the **Surety**)
3. [*name of Employer*] (the **Employer**)

BACKGROUND

A. By a contract (the **Contract**), the Contractor has been or will be appointed by the Employer for [*name of Contract*]

B. The Contractor has agreed to furnish a performance bond to the Employer.

C. Terms defined in the Contract have the same meaning in this Bond.

IT IS AGREED AS FOLLOWS:

1. If the Contractor's obligation to complete the Works is terminated under clause 12.1 of the Conditions the Surety will, subject to this Bond, pay the Employer any amount for which the Contractor is liable under clause 12.2.11 of the Conditions. If the Contractor breaches the Contract the Surety will pay the Employer any amount for which the Contractor is liable to the Employer as damages for breach of the Contract, as established under the Contract, taking into account all sums due to the Contractor under the Contract.

2. The maximum liability of the Surety under this Bond will not exceed €........................... This amount will be reduced by half on issue of the certificate of Substantial Completion of the Works under the Contract.

3. No alteration in the Contract or in the extent or nature of the works to be done under it, and no allowance of time under the Contract, and no forbearance or forgiveness concerning the Contract by the Employer, will in any way release the Surety from liability under this Bond.

4. The Surety will be released from its liability under this Bond [•] days after the certificate of Substantial Completion of the Works has been issued, except in relation to any breach by the Contractor or termination that has occurred before that date, written notice (including particulars of the breach or termination) of which has been given to the Surety earlier than 4 weeks after this expiry date.

5. The Contractor undertakes to the Surety to perform its obligations under the Contract. This undertaking does not limit any rights or remedies of the Employer or the Surety.

6. The Employer may, but is not required to, provide to the Surety a copy of any notice that the Employer gives to or receives from the Contractor under clause 12 of the Conditions.

7. The decision of a court or arbitrator in a dispute between the Employer and the Contractor will be binding on the Surety as to all matters concerning a breach of the Contract, termination under the Contract, and the Contractor's liability.

8. If the Surety is called on to pay the Employer's loss following a termination under clause 12.1 of the Conditions, the Surety may suggest a completion contractor to the Employer, provided the proposed completion contractor is acceptable to the Employer.

9. The Surety will not be liable under this Bond for a breach or termination caused solely and directly by war, invasion, act of foreign enemies, hostilities (whether war is declared or not), terrorism, civil war, rebellion, revolution, or military or usurped power.

10. The Employer may assign the benefit of this Bond, without the Surety's or the Contractor's consent, by giving written notice to the Surety.

11. This Bond is governed by and construed according to Irish law and the parties submit to the jurisdiction of the Irish courts to determine all matters concerning it.

12. [The Surety appoints .... of .... as its agent for service of legal proceedings. The Surety confirms that the named agent has been irrevocably appointed and the failure of the agent to notify the Surety of receipt of a document will not invalidate any proceedings or the service of the document.][1]

13. Money payable by the Surety under this Bond will be paid in euro in Ireland.

Given under the Contractor's common seal

Given under the Surety's common seal

Signed on behalf of the Employer

....

in the presence of

....

---

[1] An address in Ireland is required when the Surety does not have a registered office in Ireland.

MODEL FORM 7

FORM OF PARENT COMPANY GUARANTEE
(Clause 1.6)

THIS GUARANTEE is made on ....

BETWEEN:-

1. ....,
    whose registered office is at .... (the **Contractor**)

2. ....,
    whose registered office is at ....(the **Guarantor**) and

3. [*name of Employer*] whose principal office is at [*insert*] (the **Employer**)

BACKGROUND

A. By a Contract (the **Contract**) the Contractor has been or will be appointed by the Employer for [*name of Contract*]

B. The Guarantor has agreed to guarantee the Contractor's performance of the Contract.

IT IS AGREED AS FOLLOWS:

1. **Guarantee**

    The Guarantor irrevocably and unconditionally:

    1.1 guarantees to the Employer that the Contractor will punctually perform all its obligations under the Contract and

    1.2 undertakes to the Employer to fully perform the Contractor's obligations under the Contract if the Contractor fails to perform them.

2. **Indemnity**

    If the Contractor's obligations under the Contract are or become void or unenforceable then, as between the Guarantor and the Employer (but without affecting the Contractor's obligations), the Guarantor will as principal obligor indemnify the Employer against any resulting loss and be liable to the Employer for the same amount as the Guarantor would have been liable for if the obligations had not been void or unenforceable.

3. **Contractor's failure to perform**

    3.1 If the Contractor goes into liquidation, administration, examinership or receivership or becomes subject to any other form of insolvency proceedings, or if the Contractor's obligation to complete the Works is lawfully terminated under sub-clause 12.1 of the Conditions of the Contract, any such event will be conclusive evidence, for the purposes of this Guarantee, that the Contractor has failed to perform the Contract.

    3.2 The decision of a court or arbitrator or an agreement between the Contractor and the Employer will be binding on the Guarantor in relation to any failure by the Contractor to perform the Contract.

4. **Guarantee is in addition to other security**

    The Guarantor's obligations are in addition to and independent of any other security the Employer may at any time hold for the Contractor's obligations under the Contract.

5. **Continuing guarantee**

The Guarantor's liability will continue until the Contractor has performed all its obligations in full, and will not be satisfied or diminished by any payment or recovery of an amount due from the Contractor to the Employer.

6. **Guarantor's liability not impaired**

The Guarantor's liability under this Guarantee is as principal obligor and not merely as surety. Neither the Guarantor's liability under this Guarantee nor the Employer's rights under it will be affected by any of the following, whether or not known to any of the parties:

6.1   the Contractor's obligations under the Contract being or becoming illegal, invalid or unenforceable, if it would not be illegal for the Guarantor to fulfil the obligation

6.2   bankruptcy, insolvency, liquidation, examinership, dissolution, amalgamation, winding up, reorganisation or any similar proceeding concerning the Contractor

6.3   change in the status, function, control or ownership of the Contractor

6.4   death or incapacity of the Contractor

6.5   amendment to the Contract or change to the works to be done under it (whether or not the amendment or change increases the Guarantor's liability)

6.6   time being given to the Contractor

6.7   a concession, arrangement, waiver or other indulgence being granted or made or agreed to be granted or made by the Employer

6.8   anything that the Employer or the Contractor do or fail to do, including without limitation:

(1)   asserting or pursuing (or failing or delaying to assert, perfect or enforce) rights or remedies or

(2)   giving security or releasing, modifying, or exchanging security or

(3)   having or incurring any liability

6.9   assignment of the benefit of the Contract

6.10   whole or partial discharge (whether of the Contractor's obligations or security for them or otherwise) or arrangement made on the faith of payment, security or other disposition that is avoided or must be repaid on bankruptcy, liquidation or otherwise

6.11   rights against third parties that the Employer may have relating to performance of the Contractor's obligations

6.12   a reduction in, or other arrangement relating to, the Contractor's liability to the Employer as a result of an arrangement or composition under the Companies (Amendment) Act, 1990 or any similar provision

6.13   any other act, event, fact, circumstance, rule of law, or omission.

7. **Guarantor not to claim against or in competition with the Employer**

For as long as the Contractor has actual or contingent obligations or liability under the Contract, the Guarantor shall not:

7.1   be entitled to share in the Employer's rights under the Contract or any other rights or security of the Employer or

7.2   in competition with the Employer, seek to enforce any rights concerning the Guarantor performing or having obligations under this Guarantee

and if the Guarantor receives money from the Contractor in relation to a payment of the Guarantor under this Guarantee, the Guarantor will hold the money in trust for the Employer as long as the Guarantor has any liability (contingent or otherwise) under this Guarantee.

8. **No preconditions upon Employer**

The Employer may enforce this Guarantee without exercising rights against the Contractor or anyone else.

9. **Assignment**

The Employer may assign the benefit of this Guarantee without the Guarantor's or Contractor's consent. The Employer shall give notice to the Guarantor within 28 days after any assignment.

10. **Partial invalidity**

If at any time any part of this Guarantee is or becomes illegal, invalid or unenforceable, the rest of this Guarantee will remain legal, valid and enforceable.

11. **Law and Jurisdiction**

This Guarantee is governed by and construed according to Irish law and the parties submit to the jurisdiction of the Irish courts to determine all matters concerning it.

12. **Notices**

Any communication given in connection with this Guarantee must be in writing and delivered to, or sent by pre-paid registered post to the relevant party's address at the top of this Guarantee, or the Guarantor's agent's address in clause 13 below, or another address notified in writing by the relevant party. Pre-paid registered post is taken to have been received 2 days after it was sent.

13. **Agent for Service**

[The Guarantor appoints .... of ....
as its agent for service of legal proceedings. The Guarantor confirms that the named agent has been irrevocably appointed and the failure of the agent to notify the Guarantor of receipt of a document will not invalidate any proceedings or the service of the document.][1]

14. **Representations and Warranties**

The Guarantor represents and warrants to the Employer that:

14.1 the execution, delivery and performance of this Guarantee by the Guarantor has been duly and validly authorised by all requisite corporate action by the Guarantor and

14.2 this Guarantee is the Guarantor's legal, valid and binding obligation in accordance with its terms and

14.3 no approval or consent from any governmental entity or any other person or entity is required in connection with the execution, delivery or performance of this Guarantee by the Guarantor.

Given under the Guarantor's common seal

....

....

Given under the Contractor's common seal

....

....

Signed on behalf of the Employer

....

in the presence of

....

---

[1] An address in Ireland is required when the Guarantor does not have a registered office in Ireland.

MODEL FORM 8

FORM OF NOVATION AND GUARANTEE DEED

(To be used when the Contract is to be novated to a joint venture company)

THIS DEED is made on ....

BETWEEN:-

1.   ....,
     whose registered office is at .... (the **Contractor**)

2.   ....,
     whose registered office is at ....

     ....,
     whose registered office is at ....

     ....,
     whose registered office is at ....

     (together, the **Guarantors**) and

3.   [*name of Employer*] whose principal office is at [*insert*] (the **Employer**)

BACKGROUND

A.   By a Contract (the **Contract**) the Guarantors have been appointed by the Employer for [*name of Contract*]

B.   The Guarantors have formed the Contractor as their subsidiary for the purpose of completing the Contract.

C.   This deed is for the Contract to be novated from the Employer and the Guarantors to the Employer and the Contractor, and for the Guarantor jointly and severally to guarantee the Contractor's performance of the Contract.

IT IS AGREED AS FOLLOWS:

1.   **No amount due**

     The Guarantors acknowledge that no amount is due to them under the Contract on the date of this Deed.

2.   **Novation**

     The Contract is novated from the Employer of the one part and the Guarantors of the other to the Employer of the one part and the Contractor of the other.

3.   **Contract affirmed**

     3.1   Subject to this Deed, the Contract remains in effect.

     3.2   The Contractor is bound and treated as if always bound to perform the Contractor's obligations and observe the Contract as if the Contractor were and always had been named as "the Contractor" in the Contract in place of the Guarantors.

     3.3   The Employer is bound and treated as if always bound to perform the Employer's obligations and observe the Contract for the benefit of the Contractor as if the Contractor were and always had been named as "the Contractor" in the Contract in place of the Guarantors.

4. Warranty

The Guarantors and the Contractor represent and warrant to the Employer that the Contractor's duties and obligations under the Contract have been performed in accordance with the Contract.

5. Guarantee

The Guarantors irrevocably and unconditionally:

5.1   guarantee to the Employer that the Contractor will punctually perform all its obligations under the Contract and

5.2   undertake to the Employer to fully perform the Contractor's obligations under the Contract if the Contractor fails to perform them.

6. Indemnity

If the Contractor's obligations under the Contract are or become void or unenforceable then, as between the Guarantor and the Employer (but without affecting the Contractor's obligations), the Guarantor will as principal obligor indemnify the Employer against any resulting loss and be liable to the Employer for the same amount as the Guarantor would have been liable for if the obligations had not been void or unenforceable.

7. Contractor's failure to perform

7.1   If the Contractor goes into liquidation, administration, examinership or receivership or becomes subject to any other form of insolvency proceedings, or if the Contractor's obligation to complete the Works is lawfully terminated under sub-clause 12.1 of the Conditions of the Contract, any such event will be conclusive evidence, for the purposes of this Deed, that the Contractor has failed to perform the Contract.

7.2   The decision of a court or arbitrator or an agreement between the Contractor and the Employer will be binding on the Guarantors in relation to any failure by the Contractor to perform the Contract.

8. Guarantee is in addition to other security

The Guarantors' obligations are in addition to and independent of any other security the Employer may at any time hold for the Contractor's obligations under the Contract.

9. Continuing guarantee

The Guarantors' liability will continue until the Contractor has performed all its obligations in full, and will not be satisfied or diminished by any payment or recovery of an amount due from the Contractor to the Employer.

10. Joint and several liability

The Guarantors' liability under this Deed is joint and several.

11. Guarantor's liability not impaired

The Guarantor's liability under this Guarantee is as principal obligor and not merely as surety. Neither the Guarantors' liability under this Deed nor the Employer's rights under it will be affected by any of the following, whether or not known to any of the parties:

11.1   the Contractor's obligations under the Contract being or becoming illegal, invalid or unenforceable, if it would not be illegal for the Guarantor to fulfil the obligation

11.2   bankruptcy, insolvency, liquidation, examinership, dissolution, amalgamation, winding up, reorganisation or any similar proceeding concerning the Contractor

11.3   change in the status, function, control or ownership of the Contractor

11.4   death or incapacity of the Contractor

11.5   amendment to the Contract or change to the works to be done under it (whether or not the amendment or change increases the Guarantors' liability)

11.6   time being given to the Contractor

11.7   a concession, arrangement, waiver or other indulgence being granted or made or agreed to be granted or made by the Employer

11.8   anything that the Employer or the Contractor do or fail to do, including without limitation:

(1)   asserting or pursuing (or failing or delaying to assert, perfect or enforce) rights or remedies or

(2)   giving security or releasing, modifying, or exchanging security or

(3)   having or incurring any liability

11.9   assignment of the benefit of the Contract

11.10   whole or partial discharge (whether of the Contractor's obligations or security for them or otherwise) or arrangement made on the faith of payment, security or other disposition that is avoided or must be repaid on bankruptcy, liquidation or otherwise

11.11   rights against third parties that the Employer may have relating to performance of the Contractor's obligations

11.12   a reduction in, or other arrangement relating to, the Contractor's liability to the Employer as a result of an arrangement or composition under the Companies (Amendment) Act, 1990 or any similar provision

11.13   any other act, event, fact, circumstance, rule of law, or omission.

12.   Guarantors not to claim against or in competition with the Employer

For as long as the Contractor has actual or contingent obligations or liability under the Contract, the Guarantors shall not:

12.1   be entitled to share in the Employer's rights under the Contract or any other rights or security of the Employer or

12.2   in competition with the Employer, seek to enforce any rights concerning the Guarantor performing or having obligations under this Deed

and if a Guarantor receives money from the Contractor in relation to a payment of the Guarantor under this Guarantee, the Guarantor will hold the money in trust for the Employer as long as the Guarantor has any liability (contingent or otherwise) under this Guarantee.

13.   No preconditions upon Employer

The Employer may enforce this Deed without exercising rights against the Contractor or anyone else.

14.   Assignment

The Employer may assign the benefit of this Guarantee without the Guarantors' or Contractor's consent. The Employer shall give notice to the Guarantor within 28 days after any assignment.

15.   Partial invalidity

If at any time any part of this Deed is or becomes illegal, invalid or unenforceable, the rest of this Guarantee will remain legal, valid and enforceable.

16.   Law and Jurisdiction

This Deed is governed by and construed according to Irish law and the parties submit to the jurisdiction of the Irish courts to determine all matters concerning it.

17. Notices

Any communication given in connection with this Deed must be in writing and delivered to, or sent by pre-paid registered post to the relevant party's address at the top of this Guarantee, or a Guarantor's agent's address in clause 18 below, or another address notified in writing by the relevant party. Pre-paid registered post is taken to have been received 2 days after it was sent.

18. Agent for Service

[The Guarantors appoint .... of .... as its agent for service of legal proceedings. The Guarantors confirm that the named agent has been irrevocably appointed and the failure of the agent to notify the Guarantor of receipt of a document will not invalidate any proceedings or the service of the document.][1]

19. Representations and Warranties

The Guarantors and the Contractor represent and warrant to the Employer that:

19.1   The Guarantors own the entire beneficial interest in the share capital and issued share capital of the Contractor and no-one else is entitled to appoint members of the Contractor's board of directors or to vote at meetings of the members of the Contractor.

19.2   the execution, delivery and performance of this Guarantee by the Guarantors and the Contractor has been duly and validly authorised by all requisite corporate action by the Guarantors and the Contractor and

19.3   this Deed is the Guarantors' and the Contractor's legal, valid and binding obligation in accordance with its terms and

19.4   no approval or consent from any governmental entity or any other person or entity is required in connection with the execution, delivery or performance of this Deed by the Guarantors or the Contractor.

Given under the Guarantors' common seals

....

....

....

....

....

....

Given under the Contractor's common seal

....

....

Signed on behalf of the Employer

....

in the presence of

....

---

[1] An address in Ireland is required when the Guarantor does not have a registered office in Ireland.

MODEL FORM 9

FORM OF APPOINTMENT OF PROJECT SUPERVISOR FOR CONSTRUCTION STAGE ONLY

THIS DEED is made on ....

BETWEEN

1. .... (the **Client**) and

2. ....
    whose registered office is at .... (the **Project Supervisor**)

BACKGROUND

A. By a contract (the **Contract**) made on or about (date of letter of acceptance) the Client, as employer, has appointed [the Project Supervisor or ....] as contractor (the **Contractor**), for [*name of Contract*] (the **Works**).

B. This Deed is collateral to the Contract.

IT IS AGREED AS FOLLOWS:

1. The Client appoints the Project Supervisor as project supervisor for the construction stage according to the Safety, Health and Welfare (Construction) Regulations 2006, and any amendment to them (the Construction Regulations) for the project comprising the Works [and – *specify any additional scope for which this Project Supervisor is to be appointed project supervisor for construction stage, for example a process installation*] (the Project).

2. The Project Supervisor's appointment starts on the date of this Deed and continues for as long as, under the Construction Regulations, the Client is required to have a project supervisor for the construction stage for the Project, unless the appointment is terminated earlier.

3. The Project Supervisor accepts the appointment.

4. The Project Supervisor shall perform all of its duties under the Construction Regulations as project supervisor for the construction stage for the Project.

5. The Project Supervisor represents and warrants to the Client that the Project Supervisor is and will continue to be a competent person to carry out its duties under this Deed and the Construction Regulations and has allocated and will allocate sufficient resources to enable itself to comply with the requirements and prohibitions imposed on the Project Supervisor by this Deed and under the relevant statutory provisions. In this Deed, competent person and relevant statutory provisions are construed according to section 2 of the Safety, Health and Welfare at Work Act 2005, and any amendment to it.

6. The Project Supervisor represents and warrants to the Client that the time allowed by the Contract for the completion of the Works is appropriate and sufficient to enable the Project Supervisor to perform its duties under this Deed and the Construction Regulations.

7. The Project Supervisor represents and warrants to the Client that the information provided by the Client to the Project Supervisor about the state or condition of the Site (as defined in the Contract) and any premises on it is appropriate and sufficient to enable the Project Supervisor to perform its duties under this Deed and the Construction Regulations.

8. The Project Supervisor shall ensure that it is insured by insurances in the same terms as the insurances the Contractor is required to have under clauses 3.6 and 3.7 of the Conditions of the Contract, and that those insurances comply with all the requirements of the Contract, and are kept in force for the same period as required by the Contract, and include cover for death or injury resulting from the Project Supervisor's performance or non-performance of its duties under this Deed and the Construction Regulations.

9. If the Project Supervisor breaches its obligations or warranties under this Deed, or if the Contractor's obligation to complete the Works is terminated under the Contract, the Client may terminate the Project Supervisor's appointment under this Deed.

10. Without limiting its obligations under the Construction Regulations, the Project Supervisor shall give the Client all documents it prepares in the course of and for the purpose of performing its duties under this Deed (Project Supervisor's Documents). If the Project Supervisor's appointment under this Deed terminates, the Project Supervisor shall give all Project Supervisor's Documents to the Client immediately. Ownership of and copyright in the Project Supervisor's Documents shall become the Client's when the Project Supervisor delivers them to the Client, or the appointment is terminated, whichever is earlier. The Project Supervisor shall indemnify the Client against any liability resulting from the use or copying of the Project Supervisor's Documents infringing the property (including intellectual property) rights of any person.

11. This Deed is governed by and construed according to Irish law. The parties submit to the jurisdiction of the Irish courts in relation to all matters concerning it.

Given under the Client's seal

Given under the Project Supervisor's common seal

MODEL FORM 10

FORM OF APPOINTMENT OF PROJECT SUPERVISOR FOR CONSTRUCTION STAGE AND DESIGN PROCESS

THIS DEED is made on ....

BETWEEN

1. .... (the **Client**) and

2. ....
    whose registered office is at .... (the **Project Supervisor**)

BACKGROUND

By a contract (the Contract) made on or about (date of letter of acceptance), the Client, as employer, has appointed [the Project Supervisor or ....] as contractor (the **Contractor**), for [*insert name of Contract*] (the **Works**).

This Deed is collateral to the Contract.

IT IS AGREED AS FOLLOWS:

1. The Client appoints the Project Supervisor as project supervisor for the design process and the construction stage according to the Safety, Health and Welfare (Construction) Regulations 2006, and any amendment to them (the Construction Regulations) for the project comprising the Works [and – *specify any additional scope for which this Project Supervisor is to be appointed project supervisor for construction stage, for example a process installation*] (the Project).

2. Project Supervisor's appointment starts on the date of this Deed and continues for as long as, under the Construction Regulations, the Client is required to have a project supervisor for the design process or the construction stage for the Project, unless the appointment is terminated earlier.

3. The Project Supervisor accepts the appointment.

4. The Project Supervisor shall perform all of its duties under the Construction Regulations as project supervisor for the design process and construction stage for the Project.

5. The Project Supervisor represents and warrants to the Client that the Project Supervisor is and will continue to be a competent person to carry out its duties under this Deed and the Construction Regulations and has allocated and will allocate sufficient resources to enable itself to comply with the requirements and prohibitions imposed on the Project Supervisor by this Deed and under the relevant statutory provisions. In this Deed, competent person and relevant statutory provisions are construed according to section 2 of the Safety, Health and Welfare at Work Act 2005, and any amendment to it.

6. The Project Supervisor represents and warrants to the Client that the time allowed by the Contract for the completion of the Works is appropriate and sufficient to enable the Project Supervisor to perform its duties under this Deed and the Construction Regulations.

7. The Project Supervisor represents and warrants to the Client that the information provided by the Client to the Project Supervisor about the state or condition of the Site (as defined in the Contract) and any premises on it is appropriate and sufficient to enable the Project Supervisor to perform its duties under this Deed and the Construction Regulations.

8. The Project Supervisor shall ensure that it is insured by insurances in the same terms as the insurances the Contractor is required to have under clauses 3.6 and 3.7 of the Conditions of the Contract, and that those insurances comply with all the requirements of the Contract, and are kept in force for the same period as required by the Contract, and include cover for death or injury resulting from the Project Supervisor's performance or non-performance of its duties under this Deed and the Construction Regulations.

9. If the Project Supervisor breaches its obligations or warranties under this Deed, or if the Contractor's duty to complete the Works is terminated under the Contract, the Client may terminate the Project Supervisor's appointment under this Deed.

10. Without limiting its obligations under the Construction Regulations, the Project Supervisor shall give the Client all documents it prepares in the course of and for the purpose of performing its duties under this Deed (Project Supervisor's Documents). If the Project Supervisor's appointment under this Deed terminates, the Project Supervisor shall give all Project Supervisor's Documents to the Client immediately. Ownership of and copyright in the Project Supervisor's Documents shall become the Client's when the Project Supervisor delivers them to the Client, or the appointment is terminated, whichever is earlier. The Project Supervisor shall indemnify the Client against any liability resulting from the use or copying of the Project Supervisor's Documents infringing the property (including intellectual property) rights of any person.

11. This Deed is governed by and construed according to Irish law. The parties submit to the jurisdiction of the Irish courts in relation to all matters concerning it.

Given under the Client's seal

Given under the Project Supervisor's common seal

MODEL FORM 11

FORM OF APPOINTMENT OF PROJECT SUPERVISOR FOR DESIGN PROCESS ONLY

THIS DEED is made on ....

BETWEEN

1. .... (the **Client**) and

2. ....
    whose registered office is at .... (the **Project Supervisor**)

BACKGROUND

By a contract (the **Contract**) made on or about (date of letter of acceptance), the Client, as employer, has appointed [...] as contractor (the **Contractor**), for [*insert name of Contract*] (the **Works**).

This Deed is collateral to the Contract.

IT IS AGREED AS FOLLOWS:

1. The Client appoints the Project Supervisor as project supervisor for the design process according to the Safety, Health and Welfare (Construction) Regulations 2006, and any amendment to them (the Construction Regulations) for the project comprising the Works [and – *specify any additional scope for which this Project Supervisor is to be appointed project supervisor for the design process, for example a process installation*] (the Project).

2. The Project Supervisor's appointment starts on the date of this Deed and continues for as long as, under the Construction Regulations, the Client is required to have a project supervisor for the design process for the Project, unless the appointment is terminated earlier.

3. The Project Supervisor accepts the appointment.

4. The Project Supervisor shall perform all of its duties under the Construction Regulations as project supervisor for the design process for the Project.

5. The Project Supervisor represents and warrants to the Client that the Project Supervisor is and will continue to be a competent person to carry out its duties under this Deed and the Construction Regulations and has allocated and will allocate sufficient resources to enable itself to comply with the requirements and prohibitions imposed on the Project Supervisor by this Deed and under the relevant statutory provisions. In this Deed, competent person and relevant statutory provisions are construed according to section 2 of the Safety, Health and Welfare at Work Act 2005, and any amendment to it.

6. The Project Supervisor represents and warrants to the Client that the time allowed by the Contract for the completion of the Works is appropriate and sufficient to enable the Project Supervisor to perform its duties under this Deed and the Construction Regulations.

7. The Project Supervisor represents and warrants to the Client that the information provided by the Client to the Project Supervisor about the state or condition of the Site (as defined in the Contract) and any premises on it is appropriate and sufficient to enable the Project Supervisor to perform its duties under this Deed and the Construction Regulations.

8. The Project Supervisor shall ensure that it is insured by insurances in the same terms as the insurances the Contractor is required to have under clauses 3.6 and 3.7 of the Conditions of the Contract, and that those insurances comply with all the requirements of the Contract, and are kept in force for the same period as required by the Contract, and include cover for death or injury resulting from the Project Supervisor's performance or non-performance of its duties under this Deed and the Construction Regulations.

9. If the Project Supervisor breaches its obligations or warranties under this Deed, or if the Contractor's duty to complete the Works is terminated under the Contract, the Client may terminate the Project Supervisor's appointment under this Deed.

10. Without limiting its obligations under the Construction Regulations, the Project Supervisor shall give the Client all documents it prepares in the course of and for the purpose of performing its duties under this Deed (Project Supervisor's Documents). If the Project Supervisor's appointment under this Deed terminates, the Project Supervisor shall give all Project Supervisor's Documents to the Client immediately. Ownership of and copyright in the Project Supervisor's Documents shall become the Client's when the Project Supervisor delivers them to the Client, or the appointment is terminated, whichever is earlier. The Project Supervisor shall indemnify the Client against any liability resulting from the use or copying of the Project Supervisor's Documents infringing the property (including intellectual property) rights of any person.

11. This Deed is governed by and construed according to Irish law. The parties submit to the jurisdiction of the Irish courts in relation to all matters concerning it.

Given under the Client's seal

Given under the Project Supervisor's common seal

MODEL FORM 12

FORM OF PROFESSIONAL INDEMNITY INSURANCE CERTIFICATE
(Clause 3.9.6)

[Date]

To [Employer]
Re [Name of Contract]

A Dhaoine Uaisle

We refer to the above Contract.

We are the insurance brokers/underwriter in relation to the Contractor's professional indemnity insurance. We confirm that the details of the Contractor's professional indemnity insurance set out below are true and accurate in all respects.

1. Insurance Company

2. Policy No.(s)

3. Retroactive Date(s)

4. Renewal Date(s)

5. Occupation as stated in the policy(ies)

6. Limit of Indemnity

    (a) Any One Claim   €

    (b) Any One Period   €

7. The insurance includes legal liability in respect of

    (a) death, bodily injury or disease to persons (other than employees):   YES/NO

    (b) damage to third party property: YES/NO

    resulting from breach of the Contractor's professional duties

8. (a) The insurance covers claims arising out of the sub-contracting of design or supervision activities, if any, to sub-contractors/sub-consultants: YES/NO

    (b) The adequacy of the professional indemnity insurances arranged by such sub-contractors/sub-consultants has been investigated and confirmed: YES/NO

9. The insurance includes:

    (a) Liability as project supervisor for:-

        (i) design process: YES/NO

        (ii) construction stage: YES/NO

    (b) Liability under Collateral Warranties or Duty of Care Agreements: YES/NO

10. The insurance provides full policy cover in respect of:-

    (a) Date Recognition / Year 2000 problems: YES/NO

    (b) Pollution / contamination: YES/NO

    (c) Composite panels: YES/NO

    (d) Asbestos: YES/NO

11.   The amount of Policy Excess, if any, is: €

12.   (a)   Territorial Limits in relation to the insurance are:

       (b)   Jurisdiction is limited to:

13.   Restrictive endorsements/warranties on the policy:-

       ....

       ....

Is mise, le meas

Signed:

(Insurer & Insurance broker)

MODEL FORM 13

FORM OF COLLATERAL WARRANTY
(Clause 5.5)

THIS DEED is made on ....

BETWEEN

1. ....,
    whose registered office is at .... (the **Contractor**)

2. ....,
    whose registered office is at ....(the **Specialist**) and

3. [*Insert Employer's name*]...
    whose principal office is at [*insert*]...(the **Employer**).

BACKGROUND

A. The Employer has entered or is about to enter into a contract by which the Contractor will undertake to [name of the Contract] (the **Works**) on behalf of the Employer. Terms defined in that contact have the same meaning in this Deed.

B. By written agreement dated .... (the **Contract**) the Contractor has appointed the Specialist to (description of contract works or services or supply) in connection with the Works.

C. The total amount to be paid by the Contractor to the Specialist under the Contract for completing the Specialist's obligations under the Contract is €...

IT IS AGREED as follows in consideration of the payment of €1 by the Employer to the Specialist (receipt of which the Specialist acknowledges):

1. **Specialist's Undertakings to the Employer**

    1.1 The Specialist warrants and undertakes to the Employer that it has not broken and will not break any express or implied term of the Contract.

    1.2 The Specialist covenants with the Employer that, in carrying out the Contract, [the Specialist has exercised and will continue to exercise the standard of skill, care and diligence reasonably to be expected of properly qualified persons providing works, services or supply comparable in value, size, scope, complexity and quality to that required under the Contract]/[that the part of the Works to be undertaken by the Specialist, when complete, will be fit for its intended purpose as described in the Contract][1].

2. **Insurance**

    2.1 The Specialist shall maintain professional indemnity insurance in the amount of at least €...................... [[covering the Specialist's obligations under this Deed for each and every claim or series of claims arising from the same originating cause] if the Specialist is not a consultant, the following minimum level of professional indemnity insurance may be used €......................... [which may be an annual aggregate limit]] until a date no earlier than six years from the date Substantial Completion of the Works is certified under the Contract. The maximum excess shall be €....................

---

[1] Delete appropriate option. Specialists should be required to covenant fitness for purpose when a works item they are to provide is to be fit for its intended purpose.

2.2   When it is reasonably requested to do so by the Employer, the Specialist shall produce for inspection satisfactory documentary evidence that its professional indemnity insurance is being maintained.

2.3   The Specialist shall immediately notify the Employer of any cancellation, non-renewal or material reduction in the insurance.

3. Copyright

3.1   [Ownership of and copyright in all Contractor's Documents provided or produced by or on behalf of the Specialist will transfer to the Employer when the Employer receives them.[2]]

3.2   The copyright in all drawings, designs, reports, specifications, calculations and other similar documents and written information (including all information stored on any disk, computer or processing facility) obtained or provided by or on behalf of the Specialist in connection with the Works, [other than Contractor's Documents][3] (Design Information) will remain vested in the Specialist.

3.3   The Specialist grants to the Employer, and all those authorised by it, an irrevocable royalty free non-exclusive licence to copy and use Design Information and to reproduce the designs contained in them for any purpose related to the Works including, but without limitation, to construct, complete, maintain, extend, let, sell, promote, advertise, reinstate and repair the Works.

3.4   The Specialist will not be liable for any use by the Employer of the Contractor's Documents or Design Information for any purpose other than that for which the Specialist prepared and provided them.

3.5   The Specialist shall pay and indemnify the Employer against all royalties and other sums for the supply and use of any patented or copyrighted articles, processes, information or investigations required to perform its duties under the Contract.

3.6   The Specialist shall, on reasonable demand, produce to the Employer a copy of all the Contractor's Documents and Design Information.

3.7   The Specialist shall indemnify the Employer against losses, liability, damages, claims, proceedings and costs suffered or incurred by reason of the Specialist infringing or being held to have infringed any copyright or other intellectual property rights in any Contractor's Documents or Design Information.

4. Assignment

The benefit of this Deed is assignable.

5. Step In

5.1   The Employer has no authority under this Deed to issue any instruction to the Specialist in relation to the Specialist's duties under the Contract, unless and until the Employer has given notice under sub-clause 5.3 below.

5.2   The Specialist agrees that it will not, without first giving the Employer at least 28 days written notice, exercise any right of termination of the Contract, or treat the Contract as having been repudiated, or discontinue carrying out the Contract. The notice to the Employer must be accompanied by all of the information referred to in sub-clause 5.5 below. The Specialist's rights of termination (and the like) will cease if, within the 28 day period, the Employer gives notice to the Specialist under sub-clause 5.3 below.

5.3   The Specialist agrees that, if the Employer gives notice requiring the Specialist to accept the Employer's instructions to the exclusion of the Contractor, the Specialist will deal with and accept instructions solely from the Employer in substitution for the Contractor as if the Employer had appointed the Specialist originally on the terms of the Contract.

5.4   Only if the Employer gives notice under sub-clause 5.3 above, the Employer will become liable for payment of the amounts payable to the Specialist under the Contract (except for amounts due

---

[2] Include if required under the main contract (Schedule, part 1C).
[3] Only Include if assignment of copyright required.

for work for which the Employer has already paid the Contractor) and for performance of the Contractor's other obligations under the Contract, but the Employer's liability will not exceed the amounts particulars of which were given in the notice under sub-clause 5.2 above.

5.5   The Specialist and the Contractor shall, if so required by the Employer at any time, give the Employer a copy of the Contract, particulars of the amounts paid to the Specialist under the Contract, particulars of amounts due and unpaid to the Specialist, particulars of amounts remaining to be paid to the Specialist under the Contract but not yet due, and any information requested by the Employer that is relevant to these amounts.

5.6   If the Contractor's obligation to complete the Works is terminated under the contract between the Employer and the Contractor for the Works, and the Employer so requires, the Specialist shall enter into a contract with the Employer or a replacement contractor for the Specialist to complete its obligations under the Contract, in the same terms as the Contract with all necessary changes.

5.7   The Contractor releases the Specialist from any obligation to inquire about whether the Employer's rights under this clause have become exercisable, and from any liability to the Contractor for complying with this clause.

6. Notices

Any notice to be given under this Deed must be in writing and will be considered given if delivered by hand or sent by prepaid registered post to the address of the relevant party at the top of this Deed, or at any other address the relevant party may specify by written notice to the other parties. A notice will be taken to have been received on the day of delivery if delivered by hand, or 48 hours later if sent by prepaid registered post.

7. Common Law Rights

Nothing in this Deed limits the Employer's rights at law.

8. Law

This Deed is governed by and construed according to Irish law. The parties submit to the jurisdiction of the Irish courts in relation to all matters concerning it.

9. Joint and Several Liability

The obligations in this Deed of the persons comprising the Specialist are joint and several.

Given under the Contractor's common seal

....

....

Given under the Specialist's common seal

....

....

Signed on behalf of the Employer

by ....

in the presence of

....

MODEL FORM 14

FORM OF NOVATION AGREEMENT
(Clause 5.4)

THIS DEED is made on ....

BETWEEN

1. ....,
   whose registered office is at .... (the **Contractor**)

2. ....,
   whose registered office is at ....(the **Specialist**) and

3. [*Insert Employer's name*]..
   whose principal office is at [*Insert*]..(the **Employer**).

BACKGROUND

A. By written agreement dated [*insert*] (the Specialist Contract) the Employer has appointed the Specialist to [description of works, services or supply] in connection with [*name of main Contract*].

B. The Employer has appointed the Contractor to do Works, which include what the Specialist is to do under the Specialist Contract

C. The parties to this Deed have agreed to the novation of the Specialist Contract from the Employer and Specialist to the Contractor and Specialist.

IT IS AGREED as follows:

1. **Payment**

   The Specialist confirms that all money due under the Specialist Contract to the date of this Deed has been paid in full.

2. **Novation**

   The Specialist Contract is novated from the Employer and the Specialist to the Contractor and the Specialist.

3. **Affirmation of Subcontract**

   3.1 Subject to this Deed, the Specialist Contract remains in effect.

   3.2 The Specialist is bound, and considered always to have been bound, to perform the Specialist's obligations for the benefit of the Contractor, as if the Contractor were and always had been named as "the Employer" in the Specialist Contract in place of the Employer.

   3.3 Similarly, the Contractor is bound, and considered always to have been bound, to perform the Employer's obligations for the benefit of the Specialist as if the Contractor were and always had been named as "the Employer" in the Specialist Contract in place of the Employer.

4. **Warranty**

   The Specialist warrants to the Contractor that it has not breached any of its obligations under the Specialist Contract.

5. Release from Obligations

5.1   The Specialist will no longer owe any obligation to the Employer under the Specialist Contract. This does not affect any collateral warranty between the Specialist and the Employer.

5.2   Similarly, the Employer will no longer owe any obligation to the Specialist under the Specialist Contract.

6. Law

This Deed is governed by and construed according to Irish law. The parties submit to the jurisdiction of the Irish courts in relation to all matters concerning it.

Given under the Employer's seal

Given under the Contractor's common seal

....

....

Given under the Specialist's common seal

....

....

MODEL FORM 15

FORM OF RATES OF PAY AND CONDITIONS OF EMPLOYMENT CERTIFICATE
certificate to be submitted with each interim statement under clause 11.1

[*Date*]

To [*Name of Employer*]

[*Name of Contract*]

(Period of interim statement):

A Dhaoine Uaisle

We refer to the above contract. Terms used in this letter that are defined in the Conditions of the Contract have the same meaning in this certificate.

The Contractor certifies that, in respect of the work to which the interim statement referred to above relates, clause 5.3 of the Contract has been observed by the Contractor and the employers of all work persons on the Site. This certification includes, but is not limited to, the following:

- the rates of pay and the conditions of employment (including in relation to pension contributions) of each work person comply with all applicable statutory provisions, and those rates and conditions have been no less favourable than those for the relevant category of work person in any employment agreements registered under the Industrial Relations Acts 1946 to 2004

- all wages and other money due to each work person have been paid in accordance with the Payment of Wages Act 1991 and have not been more than 1 month in arrears or unpaid

- payments due to be paid on behalf of each work person (including pension contributions, where applicable) have been paid

- all pension contributions and other amounts due to be paid on behalf of each work person, have been paid

- all deductions from payments to work persons required by law have been made and paid on, as required by Law

- in relation to the employment of work persons on the Site, the Safety, Health and Welfare at Work Act, 2005 and all employment law including the Employment Equality Act 1998, the Industrial Relations Acts 1946 to 2004, the National Minimum Wage Act 2000, regulations, codes of practices, legally binding determinations of the Labour Court and registered employment agreements under those Laws have been observed.

Is mise, le meas

Signed: ....
Contractor's Representative
[*Date*]

MODEL FORM 16

FORM OF BOND – UNFIXED WORKS ITEMS
(Clause 11.2)

Bond No..............................
BOND AMOUNT: €.......................................

THIS BOND (the Bond) is made on ....

BETWEEN

1. ....,
    whose registered office is at .... (the **Contractor**)

2. ....,
    whose registered office is at ....(the **Surety**) and

3. [*Insert Employer's name*]..
    whose principal office is at [*insert*]..(the **Employer**)

BACKGROUND

A. The Contractor has been appointed by the Employer for [*name of contract*] (the Contract).

B. The Contractor has agreed to furnish this bond to the Employer as a condition of payment for certain offsite Works Items.

C. Terms defined in the Contract have the same meaning in this Bond.

IT IS AGREED AS FOLLOWS:

1. The Surety guarantees to the Employer that if the Contractor breaches the Contract or the Contractor's obligation to complete the Works is terminated under clause 12.1 of the Conditions the Surety will, subject to this Bond, pay all amounts for which the Contractor is liable under or as damages for breach of the Contract, as established under the Contract, taking into account all sums due to the Contractor under the Contract.

2. The maximum liability of the Surety under this Bond will not exceed €................................
    When the Employer's Representative notifies the Employer:

    2.1 that any of the off-site Works Items referred to in recital B above have been delivered to the Site and title in them vested in the Employer and

    2.2 the amount that the Contractor is entitled to be paid for that delivery and vesting under the Contract in the absence of this Bond

    the Surety's maximum liability will be reduced by the amount so notified.

3. No alteration in the Contract or in the extent or nature of the Works, and no allowance of time under the Contract, and no forbearance or forgiveness concerning the Contract by the Employer, will in any way release the Surety from liability under this Bond.

4. The Surety will be released from its liability under this Bond on certification of Substantial Completion of the Works, except in relation to any breach by the Contractor or termination that has occurred before that date, written notice (including particulars of the breach or termination) of which the Employer has given the Surety within 4 weeks after this expiry date.

5. The Contractor undertakes to the Surety to perform its obligations under the Contract. This undertaking does not limit any rights or remedies of the Employer or the Surety.

6. The Contractor must promptly, and the Employer may, provide to the Surety by registered or hand-delivered letter to the Surety's registered office given above or to the agent named in clause 12 below a copy of any notice that the Contractor gives to or receives from the Employer under clause 12 of the Conditions. Breach by the Contractor of this obligation or failure to give notice will not give any defence to a call on this Bond.

7. The decision of a court or arbitrator in a dispute between the Employer and the Contractor will be binding on the Surety as to all matters concerning a breach of the Contract, termination under the Contract, and the Contractor's liability.

8. If the Surety is called on to pay the Employer's loss following a termination under clause 12.1 of the Conditions, the Surety may suggest a completion contractor to the Employer, but the Employer has no obligation to accept the suggestion.

9. The Surety will not be liable under this Bond for a breach or termination caused solely and directly by war, invasion, act of foreign enemies, hostilities (whether war is declared or not), civil war, rebellion, revolution or military or usurped power.

10. The Employer may assign the benefit of this Bond, without the Surety's or the Contractor's consent, by giving written notice to the Surety.

11. This Bond is governed by and construed according to Irish law and the parties submit to the jurisdiction of the Irish courts to determine all matters concerning it.

12. [The Surety appoints .... of .... as its agent for service of legal proceedings. The Surety confirms that the named agent has been irrevocably appointed and the failure of the agent to notify the Surety of receipt of a document will not invalidate any proceedings or the service of the document.][1]

13. Money payable by the Surety under this Bond will be paid in euro in Ireland.

Given under the Contractor's common seal

Given under the Surety's common seal

Signed on behalf of the Employer

....
in the presence of

....

---

[1] An address in Ireland is required when the Surety does not have a registered office in Ireland.

MODEL FORM 17

FORM OF RETENTION BOND
(Clause 11.3)

[Date]

TO: *[Employer's name and address]*

.... (the **Contractor**) has entered into a contract dated .... (the **Contract**) with you for *[name of Contract]*.

In consideration of you making payment to the Contractor of sums that would otherwise be retained by you under the Contract, WE, ... having our registered office at .... undertake to pay to you, without further proof or conditions and without deduction or set-off, any amount or amounts up to €.................................. on receipt of your demand in writing.

Unless a demand has been made, our liability under this Bond will expire on [90 days after the end of the Defects Period].

Any demand must be in writing addressed to .... and must be accompanied by your declaration that:

- the Contractor has failed to perform its obligations under the Contract or

- the Contractor's obligation to complete the Works has been terminated under the Contract or

- any of the events listed in clause 12.1 of the conditions of the Contract have happened

You may make one or more drawings under this Bond.

No alteration in the Contract or in the extent or nature of the works to be done under it, and no allowance of time under the Contract, and no forbearance or forgiveness concerning the Contract by the Employer, will in any way release us from liability under this Bond

[We appoint .... of .... as our agent for the service of legal proceedings. We confirm that the named agent has been irrevocably appointed and the failure of the agent to notify us of receipt of a document will not invalidate any proceedings or the service of the document.][1]

This Bond is governed by and construed according to Irish law and the parties submit to the jurisdiction of the Irish courts to determine all matters concerning it.

Given under our common seal:

---

[1] An address in Ireland is required when the Surety does not have a registered office in Ireland.

MODEL FORM 18

FORM OF CONCILIATOR'S AGREEMENT
(Clause 13.1)

This agreement is made between

1. [*name*] (the Employer)

    [*name*] whose registered office is at [*address*] (the Contractor) and

    [*name*] of [*address*] (the Conciliator)

Whereas:

D. The Employer and Contractor have entered into a contract dated [*date*] (the **Contract**) for [*insert description of Works*].

E. The Contract provides for the appointment of a conciliator for the resolution of disputes.

NOW IT IS HEREBY AGREED as follows:

1. The Conciliator shall act in accordance with the terms of the Contract.

2. For all purposes related to this agreement the Employer's, Contractor's and Conciliator's addresses are as follows:

    2.1   The Employer   [   ]

    2.2   The Contractor   [   ]

    2.3   The Conciliator   [   ]

3. The Employer and the Contractor shall pay the Conciliator's fees [and expenses] as follows: *[set out agreed terms or refer to separate letter].*

4. As between themselves, the Contractor and the Employer shall each pay one half of amounts due to the Conciliator under this agreement. As between the Conciliator and the other parties, the Employer and the Contractor are jointly and severally liable to the Conciliator. If one party pays the other's share of an amount due to the Conciliator, that party is entitled to reimbursement from the other.

5. This agreement remains in effect for as long as the Conciliator continues to act in that capacity.

6. This agreement is governed by and construed in accordance with the laws of Ireland.

7. Any dispute or claim arising out of or in connection with this agreement shall be settled by arbitration in accordance with the arbitration rules referred to in the Contract, amended as required.

Signed for and on behalf of the Employer

_____

in the presence of

Signed for and on behalf of the Contractor

_____

in the presence of

Signed by the Conciliator

_____

in the presence of

MODEL FORM 19

FORM OF BOND – CONCILIATOR'S RECOMMENDATION
(Clause 13.1)

[*Date*]

TO: [*Name and address of beneficiary*]

.... has entered into a contract dated .... (the **Contract**) with .... for [*name of Contract*]. A dispute has arisen under the Contract and the appointed conciliator has recommended that €.. (the **Award Amount**) be paid to ....

Clause 13.1.11 of the conditions of the Contract provides that if a conciliator recommends payment of money, the party concerned must pay the amount recommended if the other party first provides a bond. This is that bond.

In consideration of your paying the Award Amount to the [Contractor/Employer] WE, ... having our registered office at ...., undertake to pay to you, without further proof or conditions and without deduction or set-off, any amount or amounts up to the Award Amount on receipt of your demand in writing.

Unless a demand has been made, our liability under this Bond will expire on the earlier of:

- when you confirm to us in writing that the dispute that was the subject of the adjudication has been finally determined by an arbitrator or court, which has finally determined that the [Contractor/Employer] is entitled to the Award Amount net of any amounts owed to you

- the date 550 days after the date of this Bond.

Any demand must be in writing addressed to .... and either:

- be accompanied by your declaration that as a result of the award of an arbitrator or decision of a court, the [Contractor/Employer] is not entitled to the Award Amount net of any amounts owed to you or

- be made more than 500 days after the date of this Bond.

You may make one or more drawings under this Bond.

This Bond will become operative on payment by you of the Award Amount.

We will not be released in any way or discharged by time, indulgence, waiver, alteration, release or compromise or any other circumstances that might operate as a release of a guarantor at law or in equity.

This Bond is governed by and construed according to Irish law and the parties submit to the jurisdiction of the Irish courts to determine all matters concerning it.

[We appoint .... of .... as our agent for the service of legal proceedings. We confirm that the named agent has been irrevocably appointed and the failure of the agent to notify us of receipt of a document will not invalidate any proceedings or the service of the document.][1]

Given under our common seal:

---

[1] An address in Ireland is required when the Surety does not have a registered office in Ireland.

PART III

Letters and Notices for Contractors Using Public Works Contracts for Building and Civil Engineering Works Designed by the Employer

1. The Public Works Contracts for both Building and Civil Engineering Works designed by the Employer have a common factor – they require notification in writing by contractors to the Employer and/or the Employer's Representative.

2. Such notifications may be formal notice expressed to be a condition precedent to the contractor's rights under the contract. In other cases notification in writing, is necessary to ensure communication between the contractor and the Employer's Representative and for the proper and more efficient operation of the contract conditions.

3. Under traditional contracts many situations have been encountered where the lack of a formal written has been pleaded against contractors (and sub-contractors). This can have the effect of barring them from remedies to which they would otherwise be entitled or of making it more difficult for them to secure their full contractual entitlements. The new Public Works contracts places more emphasis on formalities, written notices and maintaining records.

4. The following set of Model Letters and Notices are prepared for consideration by contractors.

5. Traditionally contractors are anxious to preserve good relationships between their clients and their client's consultants. In the commercial world that is just as important as observing contractual formalities. The new Public Works contracts require formalities to be observed. When submitting letters and notices, contractors are only carrying out what is required of them under the contracts.

Condition 1.3.2 If either party becomes aware of any inconsistency between terms of the contract it shall promptly inform the other party.

TO THE EMPLOYER'S REPRESENTATIVE

We have discovered an inconsistency between ....(give relevant details).

We request your instruction under condition 4.4 on this matter.

Yours etc.

Condition 1.5 Performance Bond

If required by the Contract the Performance Bond must be provided to the Employer before the starting date. The starting date means the date the contractor proposes to start executing the works, as notified by the contractor to the Employer's Representative under sub-clause 9.1.

TO THE EMPLOYER

Re: Performance Bond

We enclose herewith the Performance Bond as required by Condition 1.5 of the contract.

Yours etc

Cc Employer's Representative.

Condition 3.9 General requirements concerning insurances

3.9.5   Within 10 working days of a request from the employer, the contractor must provide the employer with evidence that insurances are in effect.

TO THE EMPLOYER

Re: insurances

Pursuant to your request dated ....under condition 3.9.5 of the contract for insurance details we enclose herewith copies of the Contractor's Indemnity/Public Liability and Employer's Liability/Professional Indemnity/Other (delete as appropriate) insurance certificates for your retention.

Yours etc

Cc Employer's Representative.

In addition the employer shall be informed of any reduction, cancellation, renewal or non-renewal of the insurance.

Condition 4.2   Contractor's Representative and Supervisor

Details of the proposed contractor's representative and supervisor must be supplied to the Employer's Representative

TO THE EMPLOYER'S REPRESENTATIVE

Re: Contractor's Representative and Supervisor

In accordance with condition 4.2.3 of the contract we enclose details of the Contractor's Representative/Supervisor for your records. The Contractor's Representative/Supervisor named in the Works Proposal is no longer available to us.

Yours etc

Condition 4.5   Instructions

4.5.2   If the Employer's Representative gives an instruction and call it a direction, but the contractor considers that it is a change order, the contractor shall be entitled to give notice under sub-clause 10.3 and the issue determined under clause 10. In addition to the requirements of sub-clause 10.3, the contractor must give this notice before starting to implement the instruction, otherwise it will be taken to be a direction.

TO THE EMPLOYER'S REPRESENTATIVE

Re: Employer's Representative Direction Number/reference xx

In accordance with sub-clause 4.5.2 of the contract we give notice that we consider the above referenced Employer's Representative's direction to be a Change Order. We shall provide further details in accordance with sub-clause 10.3 in due course.

Yours etc

The Contractor must give the notice under clause 10.3 before starting to implement the instruction. When providing a notice under clause 10.3 ensure compliance with the specified clause 10.3 timetable

Condition 4.7   Required Contractor Submissions

Unless the Works Requirements say that a different procedure is to apply, whenever the contract requires that a document or proposed course of action be submitted to the Employer's Representative, the following shall apply

4.7.1   The Contractor shall give the document or a statement of the proposed action and all necessary supporting information to the Employer's Representative.

TO THE EMPLOYER'S REPRESENTATIVE

Re: Statement of Proposed Action

In accordance with condition 4.7.1 of the contract we submit the Statement of the proposed xxx Works together with all supporting information.

Yours etc

NOTE

- Employer Representative may object (4.7.2).

- Employer's Representative may request further information (4.7.3).

- Employer's Representative may object after he has enough information (4.7.4).

- Contractor shall make a new submission to meet any objection given within the period (4.7.8).

- Contractor may have to submit new submissions as necessary to perform his duties under the contract and submit a programme showing his actual and current planned progress (4.7.9).

Condition 4.9   Programme

Before the starting date the contractor must submit a programme to the Employer's Representative

TO THE EMPLOYER'S REPRESENTATIVE

Re: Construction Programme

In accordance with condition 4.9.1 of the contract we enclose the construction programme for the works for your information.

Yours etc.

Condition 4.9   Programme

Before the starting date the contractor must submit a programme to the Employer's Representative and the programme will identify dates when instructions, Work Items or other things to be given by the Employer, or anything else the contract requires the Employer, the Employer's Representative or others to give the contractor. When compiling the programme an information required Schedule can be compiled

TO THE EMPLOYER'S REPRESENTATIVE

Re: Dates of Information Required

     i)   Please supply all the reinforcement schedules for the project by ……..

    ii)   List all other items

Yours etc.

Condition 4.17   Contractor's things not to be removed

TO THE EMPLOYER'S REPRESENTATIVE

Re: Removal of Items from Site

In accordance with condition 4.17 of the contract we advise you that we intend removing the followings from site ……….. on ………

Yours etc

Condition 5.4.1   …The contractor shall also submit details to the Employer's Representative of any proposed specialist, other than one named in the contract or when the contract provides other procedures...

TO THE EMPLOYER'S REPRESENTATIVE

Re: Proposed Specialists for the …….works

In accordance with condition 5.4.1 of the contract we submit details of proposed specialist xxxxx Limited for the supply and installation of the xxx works.

Yours etc

Condition 5.4.5 ....the contractor shall not terminate, allow to be terminated or accept a repudiation of such a contract without first submitting details to the Employer's Representative, except...

TO THE EMPLOYER'S REPRESENTATIVE

In accordance with condition 5.4.5 of the contract we advise you of our intention to terminate the sub-contract with xxx Limited, the specialist appointed for the xxx works. The reason for the termination is ....

We propose to replace xxx Limited with xxx Limited.

Yours etc

Condition 7.8 **Archaeological Objects and Human Remains**

The contractor shall inform the Employer's Representative

TO THE EMPLOYER'S REPRESENTATIVE

Re: Archaeological Objects

In accordance with condition 7.8 of the contract we advise you of to discovery of .... on site. We have preserved the area concerned and await your instructions in the regard.

Yours etc.

Condition 8.3.3 **Inspection**

The contractor shall notify the Employer's Representative before any work item that is to be inspected is covered or packed.

TO THE EMPLOYER'S REPRESENTATIVE

In accordance with condition 8.3.3 of the contract we advise you that ......works/items are available for your inspection. The ....works/items will be covered on ....date.

Yours etc.

Allow the Employer's Representative reasonable opportunity to inspect the works item.

Condition 9.1   Starting Date

TO THE EMPLOYER'S REPRESENTATIVE

Re: Starting Date

In accordance with condition 9.1 of the contract we advise you that we propose to commence works on ....(Date). This is the Starting Date under the contract.

Yours etc

Requirements: i)   Minimum 15 working days notice to the Employer's Representative

ii)   Maximum 20 working days after the Letter of Acceptance

Condition 9.2.3   Suspension

If a suspension that is not caused by a contractor's breach lasts more than 3 months the contractor may request the Employer's Representative permission to proceed

TO THE EMPLOYER'S REPRESENTATIVE

Re Suspended Works

Further to your instruction dated …….. reference …… to suspend the works, in accordance with condition 9.2.3 we request permission to proceed with the works.

Yours etc

Condition 9.2.3(2)   Suspension

If the Employer's Representative does not give permission within 28 days after being requested to do so, the contractor may by giving notice to the Employer's Representative terminate the contractor's obligations under the contract. In addition a notice would have to be submitted under condition 12.4.2 and sent to the Employer.

Condition 9.3.1   Delay and Extension of Time

If the contractor becomes aware that the works is being or is likely to be delayed it shall as soon as practicable notify the Employer's Representative of the delay and its cause.

TO THE EMPLOYER'S REPRESENTATIVE

Re: Notice of Delay (Number 1, 2, 3 etc A log of Delay Notices should be maintained)

We hereby give notice under condition 9.3.1 of the contract that we have today become aware that the works are being delayed/or are likely to be delayed by reason of (state cause). We also advise that we shall provide full details of the delay and its effect on the programme within 40 days of this notice.

Yours etc.

Condition 9.6   Substantial Completion

The contractor must request the Employer's Representative to certify Substantial Completion of the Works or part thereof.

TO THE EMPLOYER'S REPRESENTATIVE

Re: Request for Certificate of Substantial Completion.

We hereby advise you the works (or section of the works) will be substantially complete by .....(date). In accordance with condition 9.6.2 of the contract we request you to Certify Substantial Completion on that date.

Yours etc

Condition 10.3   Contractor's Claims

If the contractor considers that there should be an extension of time or an adjustment to the contract sum he shall provide such notice to the Employer's Representative within 20 working days after becoming or should have been aware of something that would give rise to an entitlement. The notice must be given according to sub-clause 4.14 (Communications) and prominently state that it is being given under sub-clause 10.3.

TO THE EMPLOYER'S REPRESENTATIVE

Re: Notice of Contractor's Claim(s) issued under Sub-Clause 10.3 of the Contract (Date and Reference).

In accordance with Sub-Clause 10.3 of the Contract we hereby give you notice of our claim(s) for An Extension of Time/An Adjustment to the Contract Sum/Any Other Entitlement Under or in Relation to the Contract (e.g. increased cost) (delete as applicable).

Yours etc

Within a further 20 working days the contractor shall provide

TO THE EMPLOYER'S REPRESENTATIVE

Re: Contractor's Claim issued under Sub-Clause 10.3 of the Contract (Date and Reference)

Further to our Notice of Claim (Date and Reference) we enclose the following information in support of our claim

  i)   Details of all relevant facts

 ii)   A detailed calculation and

iii)   A proposal based on the calculation of the adjustment to be made to the contract sum

 iv)   Details of the amount(s) of any other entitlement(s) claimed by the contractor

  v)   Details of the effect on programme and completion dates

Yours etc

Condition 11.1   Interim Payment

TO THE EMPLOYER'S REPRESENTATIVE

Re: Interim Payment Statement Number (...)

In accordance with clause 11.1 we herewith submit our Statement for Interim Payment Number (...). We enclose the following details for your information

- Statement showing the progress of the works

- The instalment that the contractor should be paid

- A detailed breakdown

- Any supporting details the Employer's Representative requires

- Certificate stating that the contractor has complied in full with sub-clause 5.3 (Pay and Conditions of Employment).

Yours etc

Condition 12.3   Suspension by the Contractor

If the employer fails to pay any amount due under a certificate issued by the Employer's Representative, the contractor may make a written demand for payment

TO THE EMPLOYER

Re: Demand for Payment

We write to advise you that payment of the Employer's Representative Interim Payment Certificate number (...) was due for payment on .....(date). This payment is now overdue. Unless payment is received within working 15 days of receipt by you of this demand we advise you that it is our intention to suspend the works until payment is received.

This demand is issued in accordance with sub-clause 12.3 of the contract.

Yours etc

If payment is not received within 15 working days from receipt of the demand for payment the contractor on giving notice may suspend the works until the amount has been paid

TO THE EMPLOYER

Re: Notice to Suspend Works

Further to our Demand for Payment dated.... We record that payment has still not been received. As a result we regret to advise you that it is our intention to forthwith suspend the works until payment is received.

This notice is issued in accordance with sub-clause 12.3 of the contract.

Yours etc

Condition 13   Disputes

To the Employer (Refer Section A Schedule Part 1 for names and addresses)

We notify of a dispute under the contract [DETAILS].

We advise you that this dispute is being referred to conciliation

This is given under sub-clause 13.1 of the contract.

Yours etc

notice is followed by a letter to comply with 13.1.2 for the agreement of a jointly appointed conciliator.

In the event of the parties failing to appoint a conciliator within 10 working days of the referral the conciliator shall be appointed by the appointing body or person named in the Schedule Part 1 N on the application of either party.

Any dispute that can be referred to conciliation can be finally settled by arbitration provided the conciliator's recommendation is rejected by either party within the specified period.

PART IV

SHORT PUBLIC WORKS CONTRACT FOR CIVIL ENGINEERING AND BUILDING WORKS DESIGNED BY THE EMPLOYER

NOTE

This short form of contract is for Civil Engineering and Building Works with a contract value under €500,000.

The form of contract is divided into three parts:

- Form of Tender
- Conditions (numbers 1–15)
- Schedule

FORM OF TENDER

Date...

To [*Name and address of Employer*]
For the attention of [*contact person identified in tender documents*]

[*Name of Contract*]

A Dhaoine Uaisle

We have examined and understand the attached Short Contract for Building and Civil Engineering Works and the documents listed in the attached Schedule. We offer to complete the Works on the terms of and in conformity with that contract for the lump sum of ....
.... euro (*in words*) including VAT, as adjusted in accordance with the Contract.

[*Delete from form of tender if not applicable:* We also offer to accept appointment as project supervisor for the construction stage for the Works [*add any other scope of appointment, other than the Works*] if appointed as Contractor for the Works.]

We agree that this offer will remain open for your acceptance at any time until the latest of:

* .... days after the end of the last day for submission of this Tender

* expiry of at least 21 days written notice to terminate this Tender given by us.

Your acceptance of this Tender within that time will result in the Contract being formed between us.

We agree that you are not bound to accept the lowest or any tender you may receive.

Is sinne, le meas

Given under the tenderer's common seal
....

affix tenderer's common seal

....
(*signatures of persons authorised to authenticate the seal*)

OR *(if the tenderer is an individual)*
Signed, sealed and delivered by
....

.... (*name of tenderer*)   (*signature of tenderer*)
in the presence of
.... (*signature of witness*)
.... (*name of witness*)   affix tenderer's personal seal
.... (*witness' occupation*)
.... (*witness' address*)

TENDER ACCEPTED

NOTE: Only to be signed after all award procedures have been completed, by an officer authorised to sign contracts on behalf of the Employer. Acceptance of the tender will form a binding contract.

Date...............................

... (signature)
... (name in capitals)
... (title)
on behalf of the Employer.

> **NOTE**
>
> These contracts are standard, fixed price and are not remeasurable. There is no requirement to tender a site daily delay rate, therefore there is no mechanism for using the Most Economically Advantageous Tender. There is no provision for the recovery price fluctuations.

SHORT CONTRACT FOR PUBLIC BUILDING AND CIVIL ENGINEERING WORKS

The Contractor and the Employer agree as follows:

1. The Contract

1.1.   In this Contract, terms defined or explained in the Schedule have the meaning given in the Schedule.

1.2.   This Contract is the entire agreement between the parties about the Works and consists of

- this document including the form of tender and acceptance and the Schedule and

- the documents listed in the Schedule as part of this Contract.

> **NOTE**
>
> The contract is the entire agreement between the parties about the works and consists of:
>
> i)   this document;
>
> ii)   the form of tender;
>
> iii)   the acceptance of the tender;
>
> iv)   the Schedule; and
>
> v)   the documents listed in the Schedule.

1.3.   If there is a discrepancy between this document and other documents in this Contract, this document prevails. If there is a pricing document in this Contract, and there is a discrepancy between the pricing document and other documents in this Contract, the other documents prevail. If a party discovers a discrepancy within or between the documents describing the Works, it must notify the other as soon as practicable, and the Employer's Representative will resolve the discrepancy by an instruction.

> **NOTE**
>
> In the event of a discrepancy between this document and other documents listed in the contract, this document prevails. In the event of a discrepancy between the pricing document and other documents in this contract, the other documents prevail. Discrepancies, once discovered, must be notified to the other party as soon as practicable. The Employer's representative will resolve the discrepancy by an instruction.

1.4.   This Contract comes into effect when the Employer sends the Contractor written acceptance of the Contractor's tender for the Works.

1.5.   The Contractor must construct and complete the Works at its own expense, complying with this Contract, the Employer's Representative's written instructions and the law.

1.6.   The Contractor may not assign this Contract or any part of it without the Employer's consent.

2. The Site, starting and completing the Works

2.1. The Employer must allow the Contractor to occupy and use the Site within 5 working days after this Contract comes into effect, or any other date stated in this Contract, or (in either case) a later date by which the Contractor has demonstrated to the Employer that the insurances required by this Contract are in effect. The Contractor is not entitled to exclusive use of the Site. The Contractor's right to occupy and use the Site is solely for the purpose of constructing the Works. Other limitations on the Contractor's right to occupy and use the Site may be included in this Contract.

NOTE

The Employer must allow the Contractor to occupy and use the site within five working days after this contract comes into effect, or any other date stated in the contract, or a later date by which the Contractor has demonstrated that the insurances required by this contract are in place. The contract comes into effect when the Employer sends the Contractor written acceptance of the Contractor's tender for the works. The Contractor is not entitled to exclusive use of the site.

2.2. The Employer may arrange for work to be done on the Site by the Employer's personnel or other contractors.

NOTE

The Contractor is not entitled to exclusive use of the site.

2.3. The Contractor must start constructing the Works on the Site within 5 working days after the Employer allows the Contractor to occupy and use the Site, or another date agreed between the parties, and must substantially complete the Works within the Time for Completion.

NOTE

The contractor must start constructing the works on the site within five working days after taking possession of the site and must substantially complete the works within the time for completion.

2.4. Within 5 working days after the Contractor notifies the Employer's Representative that the Works are substantially complete, the Employer's Representative will give the Contractor a certificate stating the date the Works were substantially complete, or notify the Contractor that the Employer's Representative does not consider the Works substantially complete, with reasons. The certificate does not relieve the Contractor of any responsibility or liability. The certificate may include a list of work that remains to be done.

NOTE

The contractor must notify the Employer's Representative that the works are substantially complete. The Employer's representative will provide a certificate stating the date the works are substantially complete or notify the contractor that the Employer's Representative does not consider the works to be substantially complete and the reasons thereof.

2.5. After the Employer's Representative certifies the date that the Works are substantially complete, the Contractor must complete any outstanding work promptly after the Employer's Representative so instructs. In doing so (and generally in performing this Contract after substantial completion of the Works) the Contractor must cause as little disruption as possible to occupiers and users of the Works. If the Contractor fails to comply with the instruction promptly and in compliance with this clause, the Employer may do the outstanding work itself, or have it done by others, and the Contractor must pay or allow the Employer's cost of the work.

2.6. If the Contractor does not substantially complete the Works within the Time for Completion, the Contractor must pay or allow the Employer liquidated damages at the rate in the Schedule from the day after the last day of the Time for Completion until the day that the Works are substantially complete.

2.7. The Employer's Representative will extend the Time for Completion by an amount corresponding to any delay to the substantial completion of the Works caused by any of the following and not resulting from the Contractor's or Contractor's Personnel's acts or omissions (except as an unavoidable result of complying with this Contract) or the Contractor's breach of this Contract:

- Compensation Events

- loss of or damage to the Works

- a weather event

- strikes or lock outs not confined to the Contractor's Personnel

- order or other act of a court or other public authority

- failure or delay of a person other than the Contractor or Contractor's Personnel to do what this Contract says they will do.

NOTE

The Employer's Representative will extend the time for completion by an amount corresponding to any delay to the substantial completion of the works caused by any of the following six events:

- compensation events;

- loss of or damage to the Works;

- a weather event;

- strikes or lock outs not confined to the Contractor's personnel;

- order or other act of a court or other public authority;

- failure or delay of a person other than the Contractor or Contractor's personnel to do what this contract says states.

See sub-clauses 4.5 and 4.7 for timescales for notices that must be provided by the contractor.

3. The Works

3.1. The Contractor is responsible for the safety and stability of the Works, and of all operations on the Site connected with the Works, including temporary works.

3.2. The Contractor must construct the Works according to good practice, and must only use goods and materials that are of good quality.

3.3. From when the Employer allows the Contractor access to the Site, the Contractor must

- as far as practicable, secure the Site and keep off the Site persons not entitled to be there

- keep the Site in good order and free from unnecessary obstructions

- as far as practicable, secure the safety of persons on the Site and protect them and users, owners and nearby areas from hazards and interference resulting from the Works and

- as far as practicable, ensure that the Contractor, the Contractor's Personnel and the Works do not unnecessarily or improperly

  o cause a nuisance or inconvenience to the public or users, owners, occupiers of land, roads,or footpaths on or near the Site, or

  o interfere with the use of land, roads, or footpaths.

3.4. Until the Employer's Representative issues the Defects Certificate, if the Employer's Representative gives the Contractor a written instruction in relation to the Works, the Contractor must implement the instruction. This can include an instruction changing the Works, or an instruction imposing or changing restrictions on how the Works are to be constructed.

3.5. The Employer's Representative will give the Contractor instructions that are necessary for the Contractor to construct the Works if the Contractor asks for them in writing. Such an instruction must be given in reasonable time, taking into account when the Contractor asked for it and when the Contractor needs it to avoid delay to the Works.

NOTE

The contractor must request instructions, in writing, from the Employer's Representative. Instructions must be given in reasonable time which should take into account when the Contractor asked for the instruction and when the Contractor needs the instruction to avoid delays to the works.

3.6. The Contractor must set out the Works by reference to the points, lines, and levels in this Contract and in written instructions from the Employer's Representative. Before setting out the Works, the Contractor must make all reasonable efforts to verify the accuracy of these points, lines, and levels.

3.7. Until the Employer's Representative issues the Defects Certificate, the Contractor must ensure that the Employer, the Employer's Representative, and persons authorised by them, are able to have access to the Site and other places where the Works are being constructed or goods or materials for the Works are being produced, stored, extracted, or prepared, and there to inspect, test, and observe the Works, goods, materials, and activities. The Contractor must give the Employer's Representative the information the Employer's Representative requires or requests to do this.

3.8. The Contractor must inform the Employer's Representative in good time before any part of the Works is covered or goods or materials for the Works that are to be inspected are packed or made difficult or impossible to inspect, and in each case give the Employer's Representative a proper opportunity to inspect them.

3.9. Any time until the Employer's Representative issues the Defects Certificate, the Employer's Representative may instruct the Contractor to uncover, dismantle, re-cover, or re-erect work; test, inspect, or provide facilities for testing and inspection; or any combination of these.

3.10. Any time until the Employer's Representative issues the Defects Certificate, the Employer's Representative may instruct the Contractor to remove from the Site and replace any Works or goods or materials for the Works that do not comply with this Contract or otherwise to put right (in a manner instructed by the Employer's Representative) any part of the Works that do not comply with this Contract. If the Contractor fails to comply with the instruction promptly, the Employer may do the work itself, or have it done by others, and the Contractor must pay or allow the Employer's cost of the work.

3.11. Until the Works are substantially complete, the Contractor must not remove from the Site any Works, goods or materials for the Works, or plant to be used for the Works, without the Employer's Representative's consent.

3.12. The Employer's Representative may instruct the Contractor to suspend all or part of the Works. The Contractor must, during the suspension, protect, store, and secure the affected Works and maintain the insurances required by this Contract. The Contractor must resume the Works promptly after the Employer's Representative so instructs. If the suspension did not result from a breach of the Contractor's obligations and lasts for longer than 3 months, the Contractor may ask the Employer's Representative for permission to proceed; and if the Employer's Representative does not give permission within 20 working days of being asked

- if the suspension affected all the Works, the Employer will be considered to have terminated the Contractor's obligation to complete the Works and

- if the suspension affected part of the Works, the Employer will be considered to have given an instruction to omit that part of the Works.

3.13. If the Contractor discovers fossils, coins, antiquities, monuments, or other items of value or of archaeological or geological interest or human remains on the Site, the Contractor must not disturb them, and must take all necessary steps to preserve them, and promptly notify the Employer's Representative and comply with the Employer's Representative's instructions. As between the parties, these items are the Employer's property.

NOTE

The Contractor must notify the Employer's Representative of the discovery and obtain instructions from the Employer's Representative as to dealing with the discovery.

3.14. The Contractor, and not the Employer, is responsible for the suitability and availability of access routes to and through the Site, and any required maintenance and upgrading of them, and charges for their use, except when the Contract states otherwise. The Contractor is also responsible for obtaining and providing all facilities, power, water, and other services it requires to construct the Works, other than those this Contract requires the Employer to provide.

3.15. In the time stated in the Schedule, the Employer's Representative will issue to the Contractor the Defects Certificate. But the Employer's Representative may defer issuing the Defects Certificate until the Contractor has completed outstanding work, including under clauses 3.9 or 3.10. Neither the Defects Certificate nor its deferral relieves the Contractor of any obligations.

NOTE

The "defects certificate" is a certificate issued by the Employer's Representative, under clause 3.15, and may include a list of parts of the works that do not comply with this contract.

4. The Price and payment

4.1. For completing the Works according to this Contract the Employer must pay the Contractor the Price, in instalments as follows:

- interim payments on account as Scheduled, less payments already made and any deductions permitted by this Contract

- after the Employer's Representative certifies the date the Works were substantially complete, the percentage of the Price stated in the Schedule, less (a) payments already made, (b) the value of any remaining work, and (c) other deductions permitted by this Contract

- after the Employer's Representative issues the Defects Certificate, the unpaid balance of the Price, less deductions permitted by this Contract.

4.2. When a payment is to be made, the Contractor must give the Employer's Representative a detailed statement of the amount to be paid. The Contractor must give a penultimate statement within 20 working days after the Employer's Representative certifies the date the Works were substantially complete, and a final statement of all amounts due under this Contract within 20 working days after the Employer's Representative issues the Defects Certificate. The final statement must be the same as the penultimate statement, except for amounts due for occurrences after the date of the penultimate statement. Within 10 working days of receiving a statement, the Employer's Representative will give the Contractor a certificate of the amount the Employer's Representative considers the Contractor should be paid, with reasons for any difference between the amount in the certificate and the Contractor's statement. The Contractor may send an invoice for the amount certified to the Employer after receiving the certificate. The Employer must pay the amount due on the certificate within the period stated in the Schedule.

NOTE

The Contractor must provide detailed statements to the Employer's Representative prior to a payment been made.

All statements must include a certificate from the Contractor certifying compliance with clause 7.7 (Pay and conditions of employment of work persons).

The Contractor must provide a penultimate statement within 20 working days after the Employer's Representative certifies the date the works were substantially complete.

The Contractor must provide a final statement of all amounts due under this contract within 20 working days after the Employer's Representative issues the defects certificate. The final statement must be the same as the penultimate statement, except for amounts due for occurrences after the date of the penultimate statement.

Within 10 working days of receiving a statement, the Employer's Representative will give the Contractor a certificate of the amount the Employer's Representative considers the contractor should be paid, with reasons for any difference between the amount in the certificate and the Contractor's statement.

The Contractor may send an invoice for the amount certified to the Employer after receiving the certificate.

The Employer must pay the amount due on the certificate within the period stated in the Schedule.

4.3. The Price will change only as expressly provided this Contract. The Contractor's cost of performing this Contract is all at the Contractor's risk except to the extent that the Price is to be increased under this Contract.

4.4. In this Contract, **Compensation Event** means any of the following:

- the Employer's Representative gives the Contractor an instruction

  ○ that changes the Works or constraints in this Contract on how the Works are to be executed

  ○ to search for defects or their cause under clause 3.9 and no defect is found, and the search was not required because of a failure by the Contractor to comply with this Contract

  ○ to suspend work

- the Employer's Representative does not give an instruction when required under clause 3.5

- other contractors working on the Site under clause 2.2 impede the Contractor and this was unforeseeable and not in accordance with the Contract

- breach of this Contract by the Employer

- the Employer instructs the Contractor to rectify loss or damage at the Employer's risk

- the Contractor encounters on the Site unforeseeable ground conditions or unforeseeable man-made obstructions in the ground

- owners of utility apparatus on the Site do not relocate or disconnect their apparatus as stated in this Contract, when the Contractor has complied with their procedures and the procedures in this Contract, and the failure is unforeseeable.

In the above definition, something is **unforeseeable** if an experienced Contractor tendering for the Works could not have reasonably foreseen it, having inspected the Site and taking into account all the information provided by the Employer.

NOTE

There are seven compensation events:

1. the Employer's Representative gives the Contractor an instruction:

    *   that changes the works or constraints in this contract on how the works are to be executed;

    *   to search for defects or their cause under clause 3.9 and no defect is found, and the search was not required because of a failure by the contractor to comply with this contract;

    *   to suspend work.

2. the Employer's Representative does not give an instruction when required under clause 3.5;

3. other Contractors working on the site under clause 2.2 impede the Contractor and this was unforeseeable and not in accordance with the contract;

4. breach of this contract by the Employer;

5. the Employer instructs the Contractor to rectify loss or damage at the Employer's risk;

6. the Contractor encounters on the site unforeseeable ground conditions or unforeseeable manmade obstructions in the ground;

7. owners of utility apparatus on the site do not relocate or disconnect their apparatus as stated in this contract, when the Contractor has complied with their procedures and the procedures in this contract, and the failure is unforeseeable.

In events 3, 6 and 7, something is unforeseeable if an experienced Contractor tendering for the works could not have reasonably foreseen it, having inspected the site and taking into account all the information provided by the Employer. The alternative to unforeseeable is foreseeable and therefore deemed to be included.

4.5.   If a Compensation Event happens, the Employer's Representative will adjust the Price according to this clause, but the Price can be increased only to the extent that all of the following apply:

*   The Compensation Event is not a result of an act or omission of the Contractor or Contractor's Personnel, or the Contractor's breach of this Contract.

*   The Contractor cannot avoid the adverse effects of the Compensation Event, and makes all reasonable efforts to minimise them.

*   The Contractor has complied with clause 4.7 in full.

*   This Contract does not provide otherwise.

The amount of the adjustment will be the amount of an accepted or agreed quotation under clause 4.6, if a quotation is agreed. If there is no agreed quotation, the Employer's Representative will assess the amount of any adjustment using the rates and prices in this Contract, or on the basis of those rates and prices, if there are any and they are suitable, and if not by assessing the effect of the change on the Contractor's cost of constructing the Works. The Contractor's right to an adjustment under this clause is subject to clause 4.7, but the Employer's Representative may act on its own initiative.

NOTE

The Employer's Representative will adjust the price of the contract but only where all of the conditions of clause 4.5 apply:

1. the compensation event is not a result of an act or omission of the Contractor or Contractor's personnel, or the Contractor's breach of this contract;

2. the Contractor cannot avoid the adverse effects of the compensation event, and makes all reasonable efforts to minimise them;

3. the Contractor has complied with clause 4.7 (notice of claim within specified time scales) in full;

4. this contract does not provide otherwise.

The amount of the adjustment will be the amount of an accepted or agreed quotation under clause 4.6, if a quotation is agreed.

Should a quotation not be agreed, the Employer's Representative shall assess the amount of any adjustment using the rates and prices in this Contract, or on the basis of those rates and prices, if there are any and they are suitable, or if rates and prices are not suitable, by assessing the effect of the change on the Contractor's cost of constructing the works.

The Contractor's right to an adjustment under this clause is subject to clause 4.7 (notice of claim within specified time scales).

The Employer's Representative may act on his own initiative.

4.6. If the Employer's Representative so requests before, on, or after giving an instruction, the Contractor must give the Employer's Representative, within 10 working days of receiving the request, a quotation for any change to the Price and the Time for Completion as a result of a proposed instruction. If the Employer's Representative accepts the quotation, it may issue the instruction, and adjust the Price and the Time for Completion to match the accepted quotation. If the Employer's Representative does not accept the quotation, or it is not given, and agreement is not reached, the Employer's Representative may either

- issue the instruction and assess any adjustment to the Time for Completion and the Price underclauses 2.7 and 4.5 respectively or

- if the instruction has not yet been given, decide not to proceed with it, unless it is required under clause 3.5.

NOTE

The Employer's Representative may request the Contractor to provide a quotation before, on, or after giving an instruction, for any change to the price and the time for completion as a result of a proposed instruction. The Contractor must provide the quotation within 10 working days of receiving the request.

If the Employer's Representative accepts the quotation, he may issue the instruction and adjust the price and the time for completion to match the accepted quotation.

If the Employer's Representative does not accept the quotation, or it is not given and agreement is not reached, the Employer's Representative may either:

- issue the instruction and assess any adjustment to the time for completion and the price under clauses 2.7 (Extend the Time for Completion) and 4.5 (compensation event) respectively; or

- if the instruction has not yet been given, decide not to proceed with it, unless it is required under clause 3.5 (instructions).

4.7. If the Contractor considers that under this Contract there should be an adjustment of the Price, or that it has any other entitlement against the Employer under or in relation to this Contract, the Contractor must give the Employer's Representative notice of the claim within 10 working days of when the Contractor became, or should have become, aware of it, and full details of the circumstances and the amount claimed within a further 15 working days after giving the notice. If the Contractor does not give the notice and details according to and within the time required by this clause the Contractor is not entitled to an increase in the Price and the Employer is released from all liability to the Contractor in relation to the matter (unless the Contractor's claim is about an instruction for which the Contractor was requested to and gave a proposal under clause 4.6).

NOTE

If the Contractor considers that there should be an adjustment of the price, or that it has any other enti-tlement, the Contractor must give the Employer's Representative notice of the claim within 10 working days of when the Contractor became, or should have become, aware of the entitlement. The Contrac-tor must provide full details of the entitlement within a further 15 working days after giving the notice.

Failure by the Contractor to comply with these requirements will disentitle the Contractor to an increase in the price and the Employer is released from all liability to the Contractor in relation to the matter (unless the Contractor's claim is about an instruction for which the Contractor was requested to and gave a proposal under clause 4.6).

4.8.   If a payment is not made within the time allowed in this Contract, it carries interest at the rate in the European Communities (Late Payment in Commercial Transactions) Regulations 2002.

4.9.   The Price includes value-added tax (VAT). All other amounts in this Contract unless otherwise stated, exclude VAT. Adjustments to the Price are on a net-of-VAT basis, with the appropriate sum for VAT added. For each payment the Contractor must give the Employer an invoice com-plying with section 17 of the Value-Added Tax Act 1972. If the rate of VAT changes, the Price will be adjusted proportionately.

4.10.   The Price will be adjusted by the amount of any increase or decrease in the Contractor's cost of performing the Contract as a result of a change in law after the date of this Contract that changes excise duties, tariffs, requirements for licence to import or export any commodity or PRSI, except for when this Contract says otherwise.

4.11.   The Employer may withhold and deduct any amount on account of tax required by law or the practice of the Revenue Commissioners.

4.12.   The Employer may deduct from amounts due to the Contractor any amount that the Employer considers is due, or likely to become due, to the Employer from the Contractor under this Con-tract or another contract.

5.   Representation and communications

5.1.   If the Employer's Representative is not named in the Schedule, the Employer must, promptly after the date of this Contract, appoint the Employer's Representative and notify the Contrac-tor. The Employer must notify the Contractor of any limitations agreed with the Employer's Representative on how the Employer's Representative's functions under this Contract may be exercised. The Employer may change the Employer's Representative, and must notify the Contractor.

NOTE

The Employer's Representative may not be known at tender stage. The Employer must, promptly, after the date of the contract, appoint an Employer's Representative and advise the Contractor accordingly together with any limitations agreed with the Employer's Representative on how the Employer's Rep-resentative functions may be exercised.

The Employer may change the Employer's Representative and must give notice of the change to the Contractor.

The Contractor has no right of objection to the employer's choice of Employer's Representative.

5.2.   The Contractor must appoint a representative, with authority to act on the Contractor's behalf in all matters concerning the Works. The Contractor must also appoint a competent supervisor of all the Contractor's activities on the Site, who may be the same person as the Contractor's rep-resentative. The Contractor is considered to be aware of matters (including communications and instructions) of which its representative or supervisor is aware. The Employer's Representative will send the Contractor's representative copies of any instructions given to the Contractor's supervisor. If the Contractor's representative or supervisor dies, or becomes no longer able to perform her duties, or is no longer available to the Contractor, the Contractor must appoint a replacement. The Contractor must replace its representative or supervisor if the Employer's Representative so requires because of the representative's or supervisor's misconduct, negligence, or incompetence.

NOTE

The Contractor must appoint a representative to act on his behalf in all matters concerning the works. The Contractor must also appoint a competent supervisor for all the Contractor's activities on site. The Contractor is considered to be aware of all matters of which his representative or supervisor is aware.

If the Contractor's representative or supervisor dies, or becomes no longer able to perform their duties, or is no longer available to the Contractor, the Contractor must appoint a replacement.

The Contractor must replace its representative or supervisor if the Employer's Representative so requires because of the Contractor's representative or supervisor's misconduct, negligence or incompetence.

The Contractor's representative will be provided with copies of any instructions by the Employer's Representative that was given to the Contractor's supervisor.

5.3. All communications provided for in this Contract must be in English, unless this Contract requires Irish, and in writing.

6. Contractor's Personnel

6.1. The Contractor must ensure that Contractor's Personnel are suitably qualified, trained, and experienced and are competent to carry out their tasks. The Contractor must ensure that Contractor's Personnel carry out their tasks in compliance with the Contractor's obligations under this Contract. The Contractor is liable for acts and omissions of Contractor's Personnel as if they were acts or omissions of the Contractor.

NOTE

The Contractor must ensure that Contractor's personnel are suitably qualified, trained, and experienced and competent to carry out their tasks.

It is the responsibility of the Contractor to ensure that Contractor's personnel carry out their tasks in compliance with the Contractor's obligations under this contract.

The Contractor is liable for acts and omissions of Contractor's Personnel as if they were acts or omissions of the Contractor.

6.2. The Contractor must remove from the Works and the Site any Contractor's Personnel that the Employer's Representative instructs be removed on the basis of their negligence or incompetence or that their presence on the Site is not conducive to safety, health, or good order.

NOTE

The Employer's Representative may instruct the Contractor to remove from the works and the site any Contractor's personnel on the basis of their negligence, incompetence or that their presence on the site is not conducive to safety, health or good order.

6.3. The Contractor may not subcontract the whole of the Works to one or more subcontractors. The Contractor may not subcontract part of the Works without the Employer's Representative's consent, unless the subcontracting is already provided for in this Contract.

NOTE

The Contractor may not sub-contract the whole of the works to one or more sub-contractors.

The Contractor may not sub-contract part of the works without the Employer's Representative's consent, unless the sub-contracting is already provided for in this contract.

7.   Pay and conditions of employment of work persons

7.1.   The Contractor must prominently exhibit copies of this clause for the information of persons at the Site. In this clause **work person** means a person employed by (or otherwise working for) the Contractor or the Contractor's Personnel on or near the Site.

NOTE

A copy of this clause must be exhibited at the site.

Contractor's personnel are the Contractor's:

- representative and supervisor;

- sub-contractors and suppliers of any tier; and

- Employees and other persons working for the Contractor, Sub-Contractors or Suppliers of any tier or otherwise assisting the Contractor for the works.

7.2.   The Contractor must ensure that the rates of pay and the conditions of employment (including in relation to pension contributions) of each work person comply with all applicable law, and that those rates and conditions are no less favourable than those for the relevant category of work person in any employment agreements registered under the Industrial Relations Acts 1946 to 2004.

7.3.   The Contractor must, and must ensure that the employers of all work persons, do all of the following:

- pay all wages and other money due to each work person

- ensure that work persons' wages are paid in accordance with the Payment of Wages Act 1991 and are never more than 1 month in arrears or unpaid

- pay all pension contributions and other amounts due to be paid on behalf of each work person

- make all deductions from payments to work persons required by law, and pay them on as required by law

- keep proper records (including time sheets, wage books and copies of pay slips) showing the wages and other sums paid to and the time worked by each work person, deductions from each work person's pay and their disposition, and pension and other contributions made in respect of each work person, and produce these records for inspection and copying by persons authorised by the Employer, whenever required by the Employer

- produce other records relating to the rates of pay, deductions from pay, conditions of employment, rest periods and annual leave of work persons for inspection and copying by persons authorised by the Employer, whenever required by the Employer

- respect the right under law of work persons to be members of trade unions

- observe, in relation to the employment of work persons on the Site, the Safety, Health and Welfare at Work Act 2005, and all employment law including the Employment Equality Act 1998, the Industrial Relations Acts 1946 to 2004, the National Minimum Wage Act 2000 and regulations, codes of practice, legally binding determinations of the Labour Court and registered employment agreements under those laws.

NOTE

The contractor must do all of the following and must ensure that the Employers of all work persons comply with this clause:

- pay all wages and other money due to each work person;

- ensure that work persons' wages are paid in accordance with the Payment of Wages Act 1991 and are never more than one month in arrears or unpaid;

- pay all pension contributions and other amounts due to be paid;

- make all deductions from payments to work persons required by law and pay them on;

- keep proper records as described;

- produce other records relating to the rates of pay, deductions from pay, conditions of employment, rest periods and annual leave of work persons for inspection and copying by persons authorised by the Employer, whenever required by the Employer;

- respect the right under law of work persons to be members of trade unions;

- observe, in relation to the employment of work persons on the site, the Safety, Health and Welfare at Work Act 2005, and all employment law including the Employment Equality Act 1998, the Industrial Relations Acts 1946 to 2004, the National Minimum Wage Act 2000 and regulations, codes of practice, legally binding determinations of the Labour Court and registered employment agreements under those laws.

7.4. If the Employer so requests, the Contractor must, within 5 working days after the request, give to the Employer a statement showing the amount of wages and other payments due at the date of the request to and in respect of each work person, or, in respect of work persons not employed by or otherwise working for the Contractor, ensure that their employer or the person for whom they are working does the same.

7.5. The Employer may seek information under the above provisions of this clause only for the purpose of ensuring the obligations described in this clause to work persons have been properly discharged. All information provided under the above provisions of this clause will be returned to the person providing it or destroyed if the Employer is satisfied that the person providing the information has complied with legal obligations to work persons.

7.6. If the Contractor has not complied with this clause, the Employer may (without limiting its other rights or remedies) estimate the amount that should have been paid to work persons and contributions that should have been made on their behalf, and the Employer may withhold the estimated amount from any payment due to the Contractor, until the Employer is satisfied that the required amounts have been paid. If it has still not been paid by the time the Defects Certificate is issued, the estimated amount is deducted from the Price.

7.7. The Contractor must give the Employer's Representative with each interim statement under clause 4.2 a certificate that, for the work to which the interim statement relates, the Contractor has complied in full with this clause. If there is a form for the statement included in this Contract, the certificate must be in that form. Payment due for the work covered by the statement will only be due if the certificate is given. If the certificate has still not been given by the time the Defects Certificate is issued, the portion (of the value of work that the Contractor has not given a certificate for) that the Employer determines is the labour portion is deducted from the Price.

NOTE

The Contractor must give the Employer's Representative a certificate with each interim statement under clause 4.2 (The Price and payment) for the work to which the interim statement relates, the Contractor has complied in full with this clause.

7.8.   If the Contractor does not comply with this clause, it must pay to the Employer any costs the Employer incurs in investigating and dealing with the non-compliance.

NOTE

In the event of non-compliance with this clause by the Contractor, the Employer may investigate and deal with the non-compliance. The Contractor will be responsible for any costs incurred by the Employer.

8.   Loss of and damage to the Works

8.1.   The Employer bears the risk of loss of and damage to the Works resulting from

- war, invasion, act of foreign enemies, hostilities (whether war is declared or not), civil war, rebellion, revolution, insurrection or military or usurped power

- pressure waves caused by aircraft or other airborne objects travelling at sonic or supersonic speeds

- contamination by radioactivity or radioactive, toxic, explosive or other hazardous properties of any explosive nuclear assembly or its components, in each case not caused by the Contractor or the Contractor's Personnel

- terrorism

- use or occupation of the Works by the Employer except (a) as provided for in this Contract or (b) if the loss or damage is caused by the negligence of the Contractor or Contractor's Personnel, or the Contractor's breach of this Contract.

- design of the Works by the Employer or by others for whom the Employer is responsible.

The Employer also bears the risk of loss of and damage to the Works after the Employer's Representative issues the certificate of the date they were substantially complete, unless the loss or damage is due to

- the Works not complying with this Contract

- an occurrence before substantial completion or

- activities of the Contractor or Contractor's Personnel.

The Contractor bears the risk of loss of and damage to the Works that does not result from an Employer risk listed above.

8.2.   The Contractor must promptly put right loss of or damage to the Works and goods or materials for the Works that is at the Contractor's risk. The Contractor is not entitled to payment for this except any insurance proceeds. If the insurance is insufficient, the Contractor must put the loss and damage right at its own expense.

8.3.   If the Works are lost or damaged before the Defects Certificate is issued, and the loss or damage is at the Employer's risk, the Contractor must put it right if the Employer so instructs in writing.

8.4.   Only if the Works involve alteration or extension of existing facilities owned by the Employer, the Employer bears the risk of loss of or damage to those facilities and their contents owned by the Employer caused by fire, storm, tempest, flood, bursting or overflowing of water tanks, apparatus or pipes, explosion, impact, aircraft, riot, civil commotion, or malicious damage.

NOTE

This clause sets out the insurance risks that the Employer bears. The Contractor bears the risk of loss of and damage to the works that does not result from an Employer risk listed in the contract. The Contractor must promptly put right loss of, or damage to, the works and goods or materials for the works that is at the Contractor's risk.

The Contractor is not entitled to payment for this except any insurance proceeds.

If the insurance is insufficient, the Contractor must put the loss and damage right at its own expense.

9. Indemnity for claims and damage

9.1. The Contractor must indemnify the Employer against

- claims, liability, and proceedings, and

- loss of and damage to the Employer's property (except for loss or damage at the Employer's risk under clause 8.1)) that happen in the course or as a result of the Works.

The Contractor's indemnity in this clause does not apply to the Employer's liability under this Contract to the Contractor, nor to the extent that the matter is covered by the Employer's indemnity in clause 9.2. The Contractor's indemnity in this clause for claims, liability and proceedings for death, injury, or illness of Contractor's Personnel applies regardless of whether the Employer (or a person for whom the Employer is responsible) is negligent or otherwise at fault.

NOTE

The Contractor must indemnify the Employer against claims, liability, proceedings and loss of and damage to the Employer's property (except for loss or damage at the Employer's risk under clause 8.1) that happen in the course, or as a result, of the works.

9.2. The Employer must indemnify the Contractor against claims, proceedings, and liability that happen in the course of the Works to the extent that they

- result from the Employer's negligence or

- are for property damage that is the unavoidable result of constructing the Works in accordance with this Contract.

But this indemnity does not cover claims, liability, or proceedings for death, injury, or illness of Contractor's Personnel.

NOTE

The Employer must indemnify the Contractor against claims, proceedings and liability that happen in the course of the works. This indemnity does not cover claims, liability, or proceedings for death, injury, or illness of Contractor's personnel.

10. Insurance

10.1. From the date the Employer allows the Contractor to occupy and use the Site, the Contractor must insure the Works and goods and materials for the Works against loss and damage. The Employer must be named as a co-insured. The insurance must be for the full reinstatement value of the property insured, including cost of demolition, removal of debris, delivery, Employer's professional fees, profit, and inflation during the construction and reinstatement periods. The sum insured for professional fees must be at least 15% of the Price. The Contractor must maintain this insurance until the Employer's Representative certifies the date that the Works were substantially complete, and must extend the insurance to cover loss and damage at the Contractor's risk until the Defects Certificate is issued.

10.2. The proceeds of the insurance of the Works and goods and materials for the Works (except the portion for the Employer's professional fees, which must be paid directly to the Employer) must be paid into a bank account in the joint names of the Employer and the Contractor, and paid out to the Contractor in instalments on the basis of the value of the work done and goods and materials delivered to the Site for the reinstatement, following generally clauses 4.1 and 4.2, and also paid out to the Employer for its costs. Any balance in the account after the work is done will be paid to the Employer.

10.3.   From the date the Employer allows the Contractor to occupy and use the Site, the Contractor must have public liability and employers liability insurance, with indemnity limits of at least those in the Schedule. The Contractor's public liability policy must insure the Employer and Contractor as coinsured, with a cross-liability clause. The Contractor's employer's liability policy must indemnify the Employer against the liability for which it indemnifies the Contractor, including costs. The Contractor must maintain these insurances until the Defects Certificate is issued, and after that must have these insurances in place any time the Contractor or Contractor's Personnel return to the Site in connection with the Works.

10.4.   The Contractor must place the insurances required by this Contract with reputable insurers approved by the Employer. The level of excess must be no higher than stated in the Schedule.

10.5.   The insurance on which the Employer is to be co-insured must provide that

- the term "insured" applies to each insured person as if a separate policy had been issued to each (without increasing the overall limit of indemnity) and non-compliance by the Contractor or any other insured person does not affect the Employer's rights and

- the insurer waives all rights of subrogation and other action against each insured person.

10.6.   The Contractor must comply with the terms of the insurance policies required under this Contract.

10.7.   Within 10 working days of being requested to do so, the Contractor must give the Employer evidence that the insurances required by this Contract are in effect, including copies of policies and receipts for premiums.

10.8.   The Contractor must not make any material reduction to the insurance policies required by this Contract unless approved in advance by the Employer. The Contractor must promptly notify the Employer of any cancellation, renewal, non-renewal, or material reduction by the insurer of the terms of any insurance policy required by this Contract.

10.9.   If the Contractor fails to maintain any of the insurances in the terms required by this Contract, the Employer may (without affecting its other rights) take out the insurance and pay the premiums, and the Contractor must pay or allow the amount of the premiums to the Employer.

10.10.   The Contractor bears the risks allocated to it under this Contract regardless of whether the risk is, or is required to be, insured. This includes losses and liability falling below insurance excess levels and exceeding indemnity limits.

NOTE

The Contractor must insure the works and goods and materials for the works against loss and damage from the date the Employer allows the Contractor to occupy and use the site.

The Employer must be named as a co-insured.

The insurance must be for the full reinstatement value of the property insured, including cost of demolition, removal of debris, delivery, Employer's professional fees, profit and inflation during the construction and reinstatement periods. The sum insured for professional fees must be at least 15 percent of the price.

The Contractor must maintain this insurance until the Employer's Representative certifies the date that the works were substantially complete and must extend the insurance to cover loss and damage at the Contractor's risk until the defects certificate is issued.

The Contractor must give the Employer evidence that the insurances required by this contract are in effect within 10 working days of being requested to do so.

If the Contractor fails to maintain any of the insurances required by this contract, the Employer may take out the insurance and pay the premiums and the Contractor must pay, or allow, the amount of the premiums to the Employer.

11. Property

11.1. The Contractor must ensure that goods and materials for the Works become the property of the Employer on the earliest of the following

- when they are delivered to the Site, if owned by the Contractor
- when they are incorporated in the Works
- when the Employer makes any payment for them.

NOTE

This sub-clause deals with ownership of goods and materials for the works and is particularly relevant to situations of insolvency. The Contractor is to ensure property passes to Employer on the earliest of the following:

- when they are delivered to the site if owned by the Contractor;
- when they are incorporated into the works; or
- when the Employer makes payment for them.

11.2. The Contractor must ensure that the Employer is entitled to use, copy, modify, adapt, and translate for any purpose the documents that the Contractor is to provide to the Employer under this Contract. The Contractor has no liability for the Employer's use of these documents for any purposes other than those for which they were provided.

NOTE

Sub-clause 11.2 deals with the property and rights in the Contractor's documents, which the Employer has the right to use, copy, modify, adopt or translate for any purpose in connection with the works. The Contractor is not liable for the use of the Contractor's documents for any purpose other than that for which they were provided to the Employer.

11.3. The Contractor must indemnify the Employer against claims, liability, and proceedings resulting from any of the following infringing the property (including intellectual property) rights of any person:

- anything that the Contractor does for the construction of the Works, unless covered by the Employer's indemnity in clause 11.4
- use by the Employer of the Works and goods, materials, and documents provided by the Contractor for the Works for the purposes for which they were provided.

11.4. The Employer must indemnify the Contractor against claims, liability, and proceedings resulting from any of the following infringing the property (including intellectual property) rights of any person:

- use by the Contractor, in accordance with this Contract, of documents or goods provided by the Employer for the purposes for which they were provided
- use or occupation of the Site by the Works that is the unavoidable result of constructing the Works in accordance with this Contract.

> **NOTE**
>
> Sub-clauses 11.3 and 11.4 deals with indemnifying both the Employer and the Contractor from infringement of property rights, including intellectual rights.

12. Termination

12.1. The Employer may terminate the Contractor's obligation to complete the Works on giving written notice to the Contractor. If this happens, the Contractor's obligation to complete the Works will terminate 10 working days after the notice was given, or a different date stated in the notice, and

- the Contractor must leave the Site in an orderly manner, but must not remove any goods or materials for the Works, or property of the Contractor or Contractor's Personnel used or to be used for the Works, unless the Employer or Employer's Representative so instructs

- the Contractor must remove from the Site any property of the Contractor or Contractor's Personnel that the Employer or Employer's Representative instructs the Contractor to remove

- the Contractor must, as soon as practicable, give the Employer a statement of the amount (the **termination value**) due to the Contractor under this Contract and unpaid, including in it the reasonable rental value of any property of the Contractor and Contractor's Personnel that the Employer or Employer's Representative has required to be left on the Site to complete the Works, including details

- the Employer's Representative will, as soon as practicable after receiving the Contractor's statement of the termination value, issue a certificate stating what the Employer's Representative considers to be the termination value, with reasons

- the Employer may employ others and do anything necessary to complete the Works.

> **NOTE**
>
> The Employer may terminate the Contractor's obligation to complete the works on giving written notice to the Contractor. The Contractor's obligation to complete the works will terminate 10 working days after the notice was given, or a different date stated in the notice. In that event the Contractor must:
>
> - leave the site in an orderly manner;
>
> - must not remove any goods or materials for the works, or property of the Contractor or Contractor's personnel used, or to be used, for the works unless the Employer or Employer's Representative so instructs;
>
> - remove from the site any property of the Contractor or Contractor's personnel that the Employer or Employer's Representative instructs the Contractor to remove;
>
> - as soon as practicable, give the Employer a statement of the amount (the termination value) due to the Contractor under this contract and unpaid, including in it the reasonable rental value of any property of the Contractor and Contractor's Personnel that the Employer or Employer's Representative has required to be left on the Site to complete the Works, including details.
>
> The Employer's Representative will:
>
> - as soon as practicable after receiving the Contractor's statement of the termination value, issue a certificate stating, with reasons, what the Employer's Representative considers to be the termination value.
>
> The Employer may employ others and do anything necessary to complete the works.

12.2. This clause applies if the Employer has terminated the Contractor's obligation to complete the Works because

- of a substantial breach by the Contractor of this Contract or

- a liquidator, examiner, supervisor, receiver, administrator, administrative receiver, trustee, encumbrancer or the like has been appointed for the Contractor or any of its assets, or the Contractor has ceased or threatened to cease carrying on business, or is insolvent or unable to pay its debts as they fall due or

- the Contractor died or became bankrupt or incapable of performing this Contract.

Payment of any money due by the Employer to the Contractor will be postponed, and the Employer is not required to make any further payment to the Contractor until required under this clause.

After the Works have been completed the Employer's Representative will give the Contractor a certificate of the total of the following (the **termination amount**):

- the Employer's additional cost of completing the Works compared with the cost the Employer would have incurred if the Works had been completed by the Contractor under this Contract

- other costs and losses incurred by the Employer as a result of the termination and its causes and

- amounts due to the Employer from the Contractor.

If the Employer does not begin to put in place arrangements to complete the Works within 6 months after the termination, the Employer's Representative will give the above certificate to the Contractor as soon as practicable after the 6 month period (based, if necessary, on estimates).

If the certified termination amount is less than the certified termination value, the Contractor may give the Employer an invoice for the difference after receiving the Employer's Representative's certificate, and the Employer must pay the amount due within 30 days after receiving the invoice. If the certified termination amount is more than the certified termination value, the Contractor must pay the Employer the difference within 10 working days of receiving the Employer's Representative's certificate.

NOTE

The Employer may terminate the Contractor's obligation to complete the works in the event of:

- of a substantial breach of this contract; or

- a liquidator, examiner, supervisor, receiver, administrator, administrative receiver, trustee, encumbrancer or the like being appointed for the Contractor or any of its assets, or the Contractor has ceased or threatened to cease carrying on business, or is insolvent or unable to pay its debts as they fall due; or

- the Contractor died or became bankrupt or incapable of performing this contract.

In the event of the Employer terminating the employment of the Contractor under this clause payment of any money due to the Contractor will be postponed. The Employer is not required to make any further payment to the Contractor until required under this clause.

The Employer may engage others to compete the works. After the works have been completed the Employer's Representative will give the Contractor a certificate of the total of the following (the termination amount):

- the Employer's additional cost of completing the works compared with the cost the Employer would have incurred if the works had been completed by the Contractor under this contract;

- other costs and losses incurred by the Employer as a result of the termination and its causes; and

- amounts due to the Employer from the Contractor.

In the event that the Employer does not begin to put in place arrangements to complete the works within six months after the termination, the Employer's Representative will give the above certificate to the Contractor as soon as practicable after the six month period (based, if necessary, on estimates).

If the certified termination amount is less than the certified termination value, the Contractor may give the Employer an invoice for the difference after receiving the Employer's Representative's certificate and the Employer must pay the amount due within 30 days after receiving the invoice.

If the certified termination amount is more than the certified termination value, the Contractor must pay the Employer the difference within 10 working days of receiving the Employer's Representative's certificate.

12.3.   This clause applies if the Employer terminates the Contractor's obligation to complete the Works, only if clause 12.2 does not apply.

The Contractor may give the Employer an invoice for the total of the termination value certified by the Employer's Representative and the Contractor's reasonable direct cost of removal from the Site as a result of the termination. If the Employer appoints another contractor to complete the Works within 12 months after the termination, the Contractor's payment under this clause will also include the percentage of the unpaid portion of the Price stated in the Schedule. The Employer must pay the amount due within 30 days of receiving the Contractor's invoice.

NOTE

Where clause 12.2 does not apply, the Employer may terminate the Contractor's obligation to complete the works by giving notice to the Contractor.

While not specifically stated in this clause, the Contractor should provide an interim/final statement to the Employer's Representative detailing all monies due to the Contractor, including the Contractor's reasonable direct costs for the removal from the site as a result of the termination. The Employer's Representative certifies the amount due (termination value) to the Contractor. The Contractor may give the Employer an invoice for the total of the termination value certified by the Employer's Representative.

If the Employer appoints another Contractor to complete the works within 12 months after the termination, the Contractor's payment under this clause will also include the percentage of the unpaid portion of the price stated in the Schedule (if blank, then four percent). The Employer must pay the amount due within 30 days of receiving the Contractor's invoice.

12.4.   The Employer has no other liability in relation to termination, including no liability for lost profit or contribution to overhead.

NOTE

This clause protects the Employer from any other liability to the Contractor in relation to termination, including liability for lost profit or contribution to overhead.

13.   Ethics in Public Office

The Contractor warrants to the Employer that neither the Contractor nor any person on the Contractor's behalf has committed any offence under the Prevention of Corruption Acts 1889 to 2001 or the Ethics in Public Office Acts 1995 to 2001 in connection with this Contract or the Works, and nor will they commit any such offence.

14.   Project Supervisor for the Construction Stage

Subject to the Schedule, the Employer appoints the Contractor as project supervisor for the construction stage of the Works according to the Safety, Health and Welfare at Works Act (Construction)

Regulations 2006 and the Contractor must accept the appointment in writing, in terms acceptable to the Employer, within 5 days after this Contract comes into effect, and before starting work on the Site. If this Contract provides that an individual or body corporate named by the Contractor or in this Contract is to be appointed as project supervisor for the construction stage, the Contractor must ensure that the person accepts the appointment in terms required by the Employer within 5 working days after this Contract comes into effect. If the Employer terminates the employment of the Contractor or person so named as project supervisor for the construction stage for failure to comply with the obligations of project supervisor, the Contractor must pay the Employer all the Employer's costs resulting from the termination.

NOTE

If a Contractor takes on this role and fails to adequately perform, resource and provide the necessary insurances, the Employer may terminate the Contractor's role and appoint another party to carry out the duties of project supervisor (construction stage). In this event the Contractor is replaced in this role and the Contractor is responsible for all the Employer's costs involved in the new appointment.

15. Law, jurisdiction and disputes

15.1. Irish law governs this Contract and its interpretation.

15.2. The parties submit to the jurisdiction of the Irish courts.

NOTE

Disputes under this contract are referred to conciliation in the first instance. The conciliation procedure is outlined in the Schedule. There is no reference in the contract to either mediation and/or arbitration. In the event that conciliation is not successful, the dispute is referred to litigation.

THE SCHEDULE

Clause 1.1

The following definitions apply in this Contract:

- **Compensation Event** is defined in clause 4.4

- The **Contractor** is ....
  ....(*name and address*), or as named in the attached tender.

- The **Contractor's Personnel** are the Contractor's
    - representative and supervisor
    - subcontractors and suppliers of any tier and
    - employees and other persons working for the Contractor, subcontractors or suppliers of any tier or otherwise assisting the Contractor for the Works.

- The **Defects Certificate** is a certificate issued by the Employer's Representative under clause 3.15 and may include a list of parts of the Works that do not comply with this Contract.

- The **Employer** is...
  ....(*name and address*), or as named in the attached tender.

- The **Employer's Representative** is ....
  ....(*name and address*), or an architect, engineer, surveyor or other person otherwise notified by the Employer according to clause 5.1.

- The **Price** is ....euro (*in words*) or as stated in the attached form of tender, as may be adjusted according to this Contract.

- The **Site** is the place where the Contractor is to construct the Works and anywhere else this Contract says is part of the Site.

- The **Time for Completion** is .... (*insert period*) starting on the day this Contract comes into effect, or as stated in another Contract document, in either case as may be extended under clause 2.7.

- The **Works** are what the Contractor is to complete and hand over to the Employer, as described in this Contract.

Unless the context indicates otherwise

- references to clause numbers are to the clauses of this document

- words in the singular also mean the plural and the other way around

- words in a gender also mean other genders

- **person** includes incorporated and unincorporated organisations

- references to a **month** are to a calendar month and to a **day** are a to a calendar day

- references to a **working day** are to a day other than Saturday, Sunday, a public holiday established under the Organisation of Working Time Act 1997, Christmas Eve or Good Friday.

- references to the parties are to the Employer and the Contractor

- references to a law include amendments, replacements and re-enactments

- **substantially complete** and **substantial completion** mean that
  - the Works have reached a stage of completion that the Employer can take them over and use them and
  - if there are any defects, in the Employer's Representative's opinion both (a) the Contractor has good reason for not having rectified them already and (b) neither the defects nor their rectification are likely to prevent the Works from being used conveniently and safely used and
  - any other requirements for substantial completion in the Contract have been met.

Clause 1.2

This Contract includes the following documents: (*list documents*)

Clause 2.6

The rate of liquidated damages for delay is (*insert amount*) per (*day/week/month*) or part of a (*day/week/month*)

Clause 2.7

A weather event is when a weather measurement is recorded at .... weather station for a month between the Starting Date and the Date for Substantial Completion of the Works that is shown to exceed the 90th percentile of past weather measurements for the corresponding month of the year at the same station, as determined by Met Eireann and published most recently before the day 10 days before the final date for submission of tenders for the Works.

Only the difference between the weather measurement and the 90th percentile (as so determined and published) shall be taken into account in determining any extension of time.

A weather measurement for a month means:

- cumulative rainfall in millimetres
- number of days with rainfall exceeding 20mm
- number of days with minimum air temperature less than 0 Celsius
- number of days with maximum mean 10 minute wind speed exceeding 20 metres per second.

If no weather station is named above, the Met Eireann station nearest the Site shall be used. If the station named above, or the nearest one, does not make or record a weather measurement, the station nearest to the Site that records the weather measurement shall be used.

A weather event also means the following: ....

Clause 3.15

The Employer's Representative will issue the Defects Certificate between ____ and ____ months after the date for which it certified that the Works were substantially complete. (If blank, between 12 and 13 months)

Clause 4.1

Arrangements for interim payments on account are: monthly, 95% of the value of Works completed and materials delivered to the Site with title vested in the Employer to the Employer's Representative's satisfaction.
(*Delete and replace if alternative period, percentage or arrangements are to be used.*)

The percentage of the Price to be paid after the Employer's Representative certifies the date the Works were substantially complete (less deductions under clause 4.1) is _____%. (If blank, 95%)

Clause 4.2

The Employer must pay the amount due on an invoice under clause 4.2 within _____ working days after receiving the invoice. (If blank, 10 working days.)

Clause 10.3

The minimum indemnity limit for public liability insurance is (*insert amount*) for any one event, but this limit may be on an annual aggregate basis for products liability, collapse, vibration, subsidence, removal and weakening of supports and sudden and accidental pollution.

The minimum indemnity limit for employer's liability insurance is: (*insert amount*) for any one event.

Clause 10.4

The maximum levels of excess for the required insurances are as follows:

- insurance of the Works and goods and materials for the Works: (*insert amount*)

- public liability: (*insert amount*) for property damage only, no excess for death, illness or injury

- employer's liability: no excess

Clause 12.3

If the Employer terminates the Contractor's obligation to complete the Works, and clause 12.2 does not apply, and the Employer appoints another contractor within 12 months after the termination to complete the Works, the percentage of the unpaid portion of the Price to be paid to the Contractor is _____% (If blank, 4%).

Clause 15.2

The dispute resolution procedure is as follows:

(1) If a dispute arises under the Contract, either party may, by notice to the other, refer the dispute for conciliation. Within 10 working days of the referral of a dispute to conciliation, the parties must jointly appoint a conciliator, and if they fail to do so, or if a person appointed refuses to act or becomes unable to act, the conciliator will be appointed by _____. If there is a fee for making the appointment, the parties share it equally. If one party pays the entire fee, it is entitled to reimbursement of the other party's share from the other party on demand.

(2) Each party must, within the period set by the conciliator, send to the conciliator and the other party brief details of the dispute stating its contentions about the facts and the parties' rights and obligations concerning the dispute. The conciliator may, for this purpose, suggest further actions or investigations that may be of assistance. The parties must promptly make available to the conciliator all information, documents, access to the Site, and appropriate facilities that the conciliator requires to resolve the dispute.

(3) The conciliator will consult with the parties in an attempt to resolve the dispute by agreement. The conciliator may meet the parties separately from each other or together and consider documents from one party not sent or shown to the other, conduct investigations in the absence of the parties, make use of specialist knowledge, establish the procedures to be followed in the conciliation and make recommendations to the parties.

(4) The conciliator will not be an arbitrator and the Arbitration Acts 1954 to 1998 and the law of arbitration will not apply to the conciliation.

(5) If the dispute is not resolved by agreement within 42 days after the conciliator was appointed, or a longer period proposed by the conciliator and agreed by the parties, the conciliation will be taken to have ended.

(6) The conciliation will be confidential, and the parties must respect its confidentiality. All documents provided by a party in connection with a conciliation must be returned when the conciliation ends.

INDEX

A

Agreements
    Articles of 13
    between employer/contractor 7–9
        partner/Joint Venture Member 1 10
        partner/Joint Venture Member 2 11
        partner/Joint Venture Member 3 12
Asbestos indemnities 27

B

"Base Date" 63, 81
Bill of Quantities 19, 93

C

Care of Works *see* Contractor
Change order 15
    valuation to include 83
Collateral warranties 41, 89–90
    see also Form(s); Letters/notices
Compensation Events *see also* Delay
    and Compensation Event(s)
Consent(s) 15
    see also Law
    regarding contractor 23
Contract
    see also Form(s); Letters/notices
    assignment of 20
    changes to 20
    collateral warranties 41, 89–90
    communications 35
    confidentiality clause 36
    Contractor's form with tender 98–100
        adjustments to Contract Sum 99
        substantial completion dates 98
    Contractor's programme 32–33
    co-operation with Employer 28
    date 13, 15
        defects period 90–91
        for starting 52, 86–87
        for substantial completion 90
        can be brought forward 55–56, 90
    definition 156
    delay/compensation events listed
        91–96
    disputes 175
        arbitration 79
        conciliation 78–79, 97
        continuing obligations 80
    Employer's form before tender 85
        Representative's limitations 85, 86
            documents required 86
            project supervisor 86–87
    ethics regarding 22–23, 174

Fixed Price Lump Sum 13
    no variation 64
    for Short Public Works 154, 156
        form of tender 155–156
        conditions
            compensation events 162–163
            contract 156
            Contractor's personnel 165–166
                pay/conditions 166–168
            disputes 175
            ethics in Public Office 174
            insurance 169–171
            loss/damage to works 168–169
                indemnity for claims 169
            price/payment 160–161
                adjusting 163–174
            project supervisor 174–175
            property 171–172
            rights in Contractor's documents 171
            representations/communications 164–165
            site/starting/completing works 157–158, 163
            termination 172–174
            works 158–160
        schedule 176–179
    grounds for termination 72
        consequences for Contractor 72–73
        termination breach 77
    health/safety 22
    insurance 87–89
    payment 96–97
        in full 67–68
        interim 65
        retentions 67
        time for 70
        VAT 70
    performance bond 89
    Sum 15, 18
        adjustment to 58, 82
            for compensation event 61–62
            reasons for 81–84
    terms/definitions 15–17
        are severable 20
        inconsistencies 19
        interpretation of 18
Contract Sum *see* Contract
Contractor
    see also Contract; Letters/notices
    adjusting Contract Sum 58, 82
    as/not project supervisor 21–22
    bidding for tender 98–100
    breaking substantial completion date 56–57
        delay costs 63
    claims 58–59
    confidentiality 36
    documents 15, 34, 37
        rights in 43, 97, 171

indemnity   25
letters/notices required for Public Works
   Contracts   142
management   34–35
must comply with Contract   59–60
   defaulting on   71–72
      consequences   72–74
must request instructions   159
must vouch cost fluctuations   82–84
obtaining consents   21
occupying site   44
   responsibilities   45–47, 158
passes property to employer   42
payment for unfixed items   66–67
personnel obligations
   pay/conditions   38–39
regarding work proposals   31
removal of work persons   41
responsible for care of works   24
   paying insurance   25
      for liability   26
      general requirements   26–27
responsible for workmanship/work items   48–49
safety obligations   22
sets out works   46, 158–160
starting work   52
   requiring extensions   53–54
submissions   31–32
   information request   33–34
   programme   32–33
      contingency for delays   55
   progress reports   33
supplies statements
   final   68–70
   interim   65–66
   Termination Sum   76
suspending work   74
terminating obligation   74–75
      post-termination   76
warrants to employer   22–23
Contractor, Joint Venture   20
'Contractor's Documents' see Contractor
Contractor's Personnel   15, 165–168
   quality required   38
   Representative/Supervisor   28–29
      attending meetings   35–36
   Specialist   17, 39–41
   subcontractors   39–40
Contractor's Programme see Contractor
Contractor's Things   15
   not to be removed   36–37, 159
   to be tested   48–49, 147
      for defects   49–50, 159

D

Defect(s)   15
   certificate   51
   in Contractor's Things   49–50
   minor   17

Defects Certificate   15, 160
Defects Period   16, 90–91
Delay and compensation event(s)   18, 31, 54, 58, 64,
   91–96, 162–63
   adjusting Contract Sum   61–62, 82–83
   fifteen compensation events   59
      extending completion date   62–63
   programme contingency   55
Designated Date
   contract definition   16

E

Employer
   see also Contract
   allowing access to site   44–45
   as co-insured   25
      liability insurance   26
   claims   63–64
   confidentiality   36
   co-operation with Contractor   28
   indemnity   25
   makes interim payments   160–161
      defaulting on payment to   74–75
   obtains consent   21
   owns works requirements   42–43
   random checks on contractor   91
   risks of loss/damage   24
      to facilities/Works   26
   schedule form   85–86
   terminating project supervisor   21
Employer's Representative   16
   communications   29–30
      instructing contractor   30–31
         regarding Specialists   40
      notice/time requirements   33–34
      proposed instructions   60
      suspending work   53
   decides on "enough information"   32
   determination   61
   five options regarding defects   50
   interim payments at discretion of   66–67
      deductions on full payment   67–68
      withholding tax   70
   issues completion date   56
   issues penultimate payment certificate   69
   regarding contractor submissions   31–32
   regarding delay events   54, 55
   schedules meetings   35–36
   terminating contractor for default   71–72
      at Employer's election   75–76
      referring to conciliation   76–77
Environmental Impact Statement   15

F

Fire certificate see Consent
Fixed Price Lump Sum Contract see Contract
Form(s)

of appointment of project supervisor for construction stage only   120–121

of appointment of project supervisor for construction stage and design process   122–123

of appointment of project supervisor for design process only   124–125

of bid bond   107

of bond – conciliator's recommendation   139

of bond – unfixed works items   134–135

of collateral warranty   128–130

of conciliator's agreement   137

of parent company guarantee   113–115

of performance bond   111–112

of professional indemnity insurance certificate   126–127

of letter of acceptance   110

of letter of intent   109

of letter to unsuccessful tender   108

of novation agreement   131–132

of novation and guarantee deed   116–119

of rates of pay and conditions of employment certificate   133

of retention bond   136

of tender   104–106

G

General Round Increases   81

I

Indemnity see Contractor; Employer

Insuring the Works   87–89, 169–171
    see also Contractor; Form(s); Letters/notices
    general requirements   26–27

L

Law
    Contract definition   16
    Contractor's legal obligation   21–23
    regarding consents   21

Legal Requirement   15, 16

Letter of acceptance   15
    employer to contractor   16

Letter of intent   52

Letters/notices
    for Contract inconsistencies   143
    for Contractor's representative/supervisor   144
    for discovery of archaeological finds/human remains   147
    for general requirements concerning insurances   143
    for notifying Employer delay in completion   148
    for notifying Employer of dispute   151
    for perceiving "instruction" as change order   144
    for performance bond   143
    for proposing starting date   148
    for providing notice of Contractor's claims   149
    for removing items from site   146

for requesting certificate of substantial completion   149

for requesting permission from Employer to proceed   148

for required Contractor submissions   145

for submitting Contractor's programme   145–146

for submitting interim payment statement   150

for submitting items for inspection   147

for submitting specialist's details   146

for suspension of work by Contractor   150

for termination by Contractor   147, 148

Liability
    broad definition   26

M

Met Éireann   93

"Most Economically Advantageous Tender"   100

P

Performance Bond   19, 89
    see also Form(s); Letters/notices

Perils insurance policies   26

Planning permission see Consent

Pricing Document   18
    doesn't limit contractor's obligations   19

Professional indemnity insurance   26

Project supervisor   21, 86–87, 174–175
    see also Form(s); Letters/notices
    whether contractor or not   22

Property
    infringement of rights   42

Proposed instructions see Employer's Representative

Proven Cost Method (PV1)
    price variation   63

Public Works Contracts
    letters/notices required   142

R

Risk items   24
    insurance of   25

S

Safety file   22

Section
    contract definition   16

Site   44
    see also Contractor; Letters/notices
    access routes   47
    archaeological objects/human remains   46–47, 96, 160
    contract definition   16
    safety/security   45–46
    trespassers   45

Site Working Day
    contract definition   16–17

Specialist
   see also Letters/notices
   contract definition   17
Subcontractor   17, 39–40
"Substantial Completion" date   18, 56
   brought forward   90
   certificate for   21, 56
   contract definition   17
   if missed   56–57
      delay costs   62–63

T

Tender price   13
Terrorism indemnities   27

V

Valued Added Tax (VAT)   70
   contract definition   17

W

Weather event   93
Workers
   definition of   81
   wages/expenses
      increase/decrease   81
Working day   18
Works Items   15, 37
   see also Defect(s)
   contract definition   17
   ownership of   42
   quality of   48
      inspection of   48–49
   supplier of   17
   unfixed   66–67
Works proposal   18, 31
   doesn't limit contractor's obligations   19
Works Requirements   15, 18, 42
   regarding site   44